ROB GION, JR.

Redefining
INTIMACY

DEVELOPING INTIMATE RELATIONSHIPS
WITH GOD AND OTHERS

INTIMACY
PUBLISHING

This book is a work of nonfiction. It traces the personal story of the author and his understanding of the subject of intimacy. Except for the author's immediate family, all names of individuals referenced throughout the book have been changed to protect their identities. All stories and events in this book actually happened.

The content of this book is for informational purposes only and is not intended to serve as a substitute for consultation with a qualified health-care provider. For matters regarding your mental and physical health, please seek the advice of a physician or other health-care provider. Neither the author nor the publisher shall be liable or responsible for any loss or damage allegedly arising from any information or suggestion in this book.

Unless otherwise noted, all Scripture quotations are from the ESV® Bible (*The Holy Bible, English Standard Version®*), copyright © 2001 by Crossway Bibles, a publishing ministry of Good News Publishers. Used by permission. All rights reserved.

First paperback edition September 2024

Book design by Rosemary Strohm
Developmental editing and line editing by Michelle Schacht
Copyediting and proofreading by Beth Bazar

ISBN 979-8-9904407-0-8 (paperback)
ISBN 979-8-9904407-2-2 (hardback)
ISBN 979-8-9904407-1-5 (e-book)

Published by Intimacy Publishing
www.intimacypublishing.com

Acknowledgments

This book would not exist apart from the help and support of many individuals. There is no way to adequately thank everyone who really should be thanked on this page. However, I would like to recognize some of the people who were most instrumental in the production of this book.

First, without God and His divine work and redemption in my life, I would have no hope of ever communicating anything on this topic. I give all thanks and glory to God first and foremost for all things, including this book's publication.

Second, the grace, love, forgiveness, support, and ongoing encouragement from my lovely wife, Tammy, is incredible. Frankly, it's supernatural and occurs because of Tammy's connection with God. Sweetie, I love you more than words can share and am so thankful for you. In addition, my children, Aaron and Emma, have been not only a loving support and encouragement to me but a blessing. Through my years of not walking in intimacy, I was not the dad I could have been. I'm grateful for their forgiveness, acceptance, and love, and I'm super-grateful we have truly intimate relationships today.

Next, I'd like to thank FirstLight Ministries (www.firstlightstlouis.org) for helping me early on in my process of addiction recovery. Sean and David, thank you for the ongoing work you do to help others. Along with

FirstLight and its leadership, over the past nine years I have been able to establish close relationships with many men who have trusted me with their stories and their brokenness. I value each of you, and the level of intimacy we've shared has helped me. A special note of thanks goes out to my dear friend Mike O'Dea. You have been a mentor, support partner, and encourager to me over the past ten years. Everyone needs a friend like you in their life.

Finally, after honing this manuscript to a condition close to being ready to publish, I've had tremendous support to get it where it is today. Thank you to my friends who have read samples and given feedback. This includes the invaluable support I received in my Life Group. Thank you so much to both Michelle Schacht and Beth Bazar, who did a great job in the editing process. I highly value your professional work. Beth, especially, went above and beyond, closely connecting with my writing and lending extremely valuable guidance. You were terrific to work with, and I can't thank you enough! Finally, thank you so much to Rosemary Strohm for your outstanding work in designing the cover and the interior formatting of the book. You all did an excellent job and are so appreciated.

CONTENTS

Introduction

It may sound strange to ask the question, What is intimacy? I bet most of us think we have a pretty solid understanding of the word. Isn't it really all about sex? That's where our minds naturally go. After all, men and women alike say things like "We were intimate last night" when discussing having sex with their partner. But what if we are wrong about our understanding or have examined the term with a limited view? Does the word itself mean something different when describing a relationship between a husband and wife than when speaking of a college student and her best friend? It certainly seems like it does. How can we go about redefining intimacy to fully grasp all that God intended and then apply that definition to dramatically improve every relationship in our lives? Does it even matter if we can?

These are questions worth considering. Nine years ago, I *thought* I understood intimacy. I emphasize the word *thought* because, in truth, I didn't have a clue about what intimacy was. My life was a mess back then because I was hiding so much from others that no one really knew the real me. I had never shared with anyone that I was a victim of physical, emotional, and sexual abuse as a child. No one knew that despite the act I projected of having everything together, I could hardly get through the day without the use of porn or sex, which was my drug of choice to get me through. And because I feared what others might think of me or what might happen if they knew the real me, I didn't allow them into my life. Therefore, no one could help me process my past hurts or help me realize I didn't need my drug.

Although I had been married almost twenty years at that time, the word *intimacy* didn't apply to my relationship with my wife. I knew the truth about myself, my past, and my need for a coping vice. But she didn't know about any of that. She didn't know the real me. It was at this point that I hit rock bottom and finally sought the help I needed. My years of hiding, lying, and living in ways I knew were wrong brought me to a place where I simply couldn't live with myself any longer. If I wasn't suicidal, I was close to it. Something had to change.

I first learned of the term *intimacy disorder* when my personal therapist told me, "Rob, you have an intimacy disorder." That sentence launched me on a path of discovery. I needed to understand what real intimacy was and how I could make tangible changes in my life to experience that intimacy in all my relationships, especially my marital relationship. As I embraced that process, I realized I was not alone in my misunderstanding of the concept.

Now, you might reasonably ask, "Who are you, and why should I listen?" I confess I'm not all that notable. I don't have a platform. I'm just an average guy. But I'm an average guy who has lived most of his life *without* experiencing intimate relationships. That's despite the fact that, at the time of writing this book, I've been married for more than twenty-eight years. And it's despite the fact that as an ordained pastor who served bivocationally in the pulpit weekly for more than three years, I was not in a truly intimate relationship with the Lord. But all this radically changed nine years ago when I redefined intimacy and took it back for myself, building a life centered on intimate relationships. Now, I teach and coach others how to do so.

I have three primary goals in writing this book. First, I want to answer the big question raised in the opening paragraph. My conviction is that few people are living life in very intimate relationships, and part of the problem is that we haven't defined what real intimacy is and how to achieve it. Worse, I believe improper understandings of intimacy are leading people away from intimate relationships rather than toward them.

I want you to get the most out of life, and I believe that will occur when you ground yourself in truly intimate relationships. Intimacy itself is the deepest longing human beings share; it is essential to our nature and survival. God designed us with intimacy in mind. In fact, I'm convinced that God desires, more than anything else, an intimate love relationship with each of us.

Second, in sharing my story, I want to illustrate the factors that led to my intimacy problems. My invitation is for you to walk with me for a bit to see where I was and how I got there. I'm hoping certain things I've experienced and learned will connect with your story. I'll let you determine whether applying those truths and avoiding those snares would make a difference in your relationships. I want you to come away from reading this book with actionable tools and behaviors you can employ to help your relationships become more intimate. For those reading this who have recently learned they have an intimacy disorder and perhaps haven't ever experienced truly intimate relationships, I'm hoping you'll learn how to redirect your path.

I must warn you there is a lot of hurt and brokenness in my story. Traumatic events, like those just mentioned, have befallen me, and I've done my share of hurtful things to both myself and others. Yet these things shaped who I am and help explain why I had genuine issues with understanding intimacy. In sharing my hurts and the difficult things that happened to me, I am not trying to shift blame for my mistakes. I'm also not seeking to excuse the terrible things I've done in my life. But context is important. This is never truer than when we examine ourselves and how we've arrived at the place where we are. It's also important to understand that our past does not need to define our future.

Finally, and maybe most importantly, I hope to encourage you that life-altering intimacy is possible. It seems hope is in short supply in our world today. It would bless me if you came away with hope for yourself and those close to you. Maybe what you need right now, more than anything else, is a spark or a push to get you beyond where you currently are. I pray this book provides just that.

AUTHOR'S NOTE

At the end of each chapter, you'll see this little icon with a "next step" for you to consider. These are ideas for applying the information provided in the chapter to your situation. For the introduction, my next-step recommendation is for you to commit to growing in intimacy.

One quick and easy way to do that is by becoming an "Intimacy Fan" (a.k.a. subscriber) at **www.RedefiningIntimacy.org**. It's completely free, and you won't be spammed or ever have your email address shared with others. You'll receive a biweekly email from me with a practical step for the week to help your relationships grow to be more intimate. I promise to keep it to no more than a three-to-five-minute read each week.

CHAPTER 1

Redefining Terms

Everything starts with developing a better understanding of what is this thing called intimacy. When my counselor said I had an intimacy disorder, I quickly did all I could to fix it. I'm the type of guy that when a problem presents itself, I want to solve it, and preferably as fast as I can. The need to "fix things" seems to be a trait of many men, and I'm certainly no exception. If I have a problem, I want to know all I can about the nature of it. So, upon learning about my disorder, I asked my counselor what were the best books I could read to understand both intimacy and my challenge with it.

In short order, I purchased several books. I wanted help, and I wanted to learn. Some of the books I read early on were incredibly helpful, and I'm grateful to those authors. But most of the books were directly related to addiction or overcoming trauma and abuse. (I believe most humans suffering from an intimacy disorder are addicted to something to compensate for the lack of intimacy. For most, it's sex or some aspect of sex, including pornography, masturbation, or other outlets that produce the endorphins intimate relationships usually provide.) While these books were helpful in overcoming my addiction, they barely touched the surface when it came to helping me understand intimacy. They alluded to it, but none of the books gave a clear definition of the concept. So, I wrote one.

Even at this point in reading, you probably don't have a clue what I'm talking about when I say "intimacy" or "intimate." Before reading any further, take a moment and mentally answer the question for yourself. What is intimacy?

Here's how the online *Merriam-Webster* dictionary defines it:[1]

1. the state of being intimate: familiarity

2. something of a personal or private nature

The same dictionary offers the following definitions of *intimate*:[2]

---

[1]   *Merriam-Webster*, s.v. "intimacy," accessed June 14, 2024, https://www.merriam-webster.com/dictionary/intimacy.

[2]   *Merriam-Webster*, s.v. "intimate," accessed June 14, 2024, https://www.merriam-webster.com/dictionary/intimate.

Noun: a very close friend or confidant

Adjective:

1. a. marked by a warm friendship developing through long association

   b. suggesting informal warmth or privacy

   c. engaged in, involving, or marked by sex or sexual relations

2. of a very personal or private nature

3. marked by very close association, contact, or familiarity

4. a. intrinsic, essential

   b. belonging to or characterizing one's deepest nature

With the exception of definition 1.c., I like these better than the quick Google search definition, which reads: "close familiarity or friendship; closeness. A private, cozy atmosphere. An intimate act, especially sexual intercourse." However, I believe none of these definitions capture the heart of what real intimacy is. They don't get to the spiritual side of intimacy because they don't address what's involved in intimacy. For example, how does one define a "very close friend"? That is likely different for everyone. Further, these definitions miss the point because they don't get to the root of how intimacy occurs and what prerequisites and actions are needed for intimacy to exist.

So, if you and I are going to understand intimacy, we must better understand what intimacy is and is not.

As already stated, it's not sexual intercourse. That would be way too simple, and frankly, it would pollute the word. Nine years ago, *sex* and *intimacy* for me were synonymous. But people have sex all the time and there is no intimacy in the act. In fact, somewhere over the past ten to fifteen years, we have coined a new term: *hooking up*. In case you don't know it or have been living under a rock like I was, *hooking up* means meeting for casual sex (at least that's what it means at the time when this book is being published).

Further, it is very possible for a husband and wife to be intimate with each other while not being sexual. Without sex, husbands and wives can share very close, very intimate times when they are known by each other. A special closeness can occur without sex. A mutual understanding and respect for each other is not dependent on sex. Please don't get me wrong, I thoroughly enjoy being sexual with my wife. But I have learned that we can have amazing times of intimacy during which we are closely connected, meeting each other's needs, and being one relationally—all while fully clothed.

I also don't think the idea of simple "warmth or privacy" is enough to define intimacy. I would say my wife has made our home a very warm, private, and cozy place. And yet we lacked real intimacy for years despite the wonderful abode we had. There's nothing wrong with working tirelessly to design an atmosphere where you hope intimacy takes place. In fact, a certain amount of effort to arrange an atmosphere for intimacy is important. Yet you cannot make intimacy occur by creating settings conducive to it. A specific setting or outward appearance does not define or produce intimacy.

So, then, what is intimacy if it is not all that? Here's my definition, and throughout the rest of this book, this is what I mean by intimacy:

Intimacy is the natural outcome of relationships in which certainty exists between both parties that each person is consistently

- working to know their true self at their core and to be this true self in the presence of the other party, hiding nothing and putting themselves in a vulnerable position;

- aware that they are loved and cared for exactly as they are, inclusive of their own faults, wrinkles, and problems;

- living, loving, and interacting within an atmosphere of ongoing and mutual forgiveness and acceptance;

- expressing and openly sharing feelings because the fear of rejection is nonexistent; and

- feeling a regular and consistent closeness that is unique and special—a closeness not shared with anyone else.

I realize my definition is not simple or short. But intimacy is not simple either, nor is it something easy to achieve. It does often take "long association," as *Merriam-Webster* puts it. It takes work, usually hard work. Intimacy always requires a willingness to be open, which is something we, by nature, frequently don't want to do because we open ourselves to the possibility of being hurt.

Note that my definition does not require sex. In fact, it doesn't even mention sex. I believe sex may well be a natural and appropriate by-product of intimacy between a man and woman in a committed relationship, but sex has little to do with intimacy itself. Drs. Les and Leslie Parrott in their fabulous book *Saving Your Marriage before It Starts* discuss what they call the Anatomy of Love. They describe a triangular model of love, which was developed by the excellent work of Yale University psychologist Robert Sternberg. This model is helpful in defining not only love but also intimacy. In this model, intimacy is one of three interdependent legs of love. Passion and commitment are the other two legs. Passion may include sex, but as the Parrotts well state, "Intimacy fills our heart's deepest longings for closeness and acceptance."[3] If you think about marital love as sitting on a three-legged stool, you can easily see that the stool won't stand without one of the legs. Yet, while marital love requires the three legs, and the legs are connected in supporting the seat of the stool, neither

---

[3]   Les Parrott and Leslie Parrott, *Saving Your Marriage before It Starts* (Grand Rapids, MI: Zondervan, 2006), 37–40.

the intimacy leg nor the commitment leg needs sex in order to exist on its own.

Note, too, that my definition also does not specifically require a relationship between a man and a woman. Intimacy can and should occur between a man and his son. It should also occur between a mother and her daughter. Further, it is highly possible for two close friends to experience a great deal of intimacy. In fact, I would say you don't really have a close friend unless you have a significant degree of intimacy with him or her.

Additionally, while intimacy always requires a relationship between people, it can also occur in a group rather than just between two. For example, I experienced intimacy like this recently in a men's small-group Bible study. In this circle, I was hurting because of circumstances in my life that reminded me of parts of my past that were embarrassing and hurtful. Because of the trust I have in the men of my group and my desire to be authentic and transparent with them, I shared a very delicate part of my story. I received much love and support; their acceptance and affection showed that intimacy existed.

Moving onward, there are a few more things that are essential to understand. First, the result of intimacy is always security and closeness. In the study group, my openness prompted another man to share a similar experience and hurt. As he described the situation, he said, "That happened some thirty years ago, and I have told no one about it." In our circle, he felt a sense of relief that he could speak about his hurt and embarrassment and reveal who he really was while still being fully accepted. That's what happens when intimacy is present. We can share because we are loved, accepted, and confident that we can truly trust another human being. What's heartbreaking to me is how few people have relationships like I just described, ones defined by intimacy.

The second essential point is that intimacy can never occur where hiding is present. The truth is, many of us learn at an early age to hide. In fact, hide-and-seek might be one of the most popular children's games around. But sadly, for many children, hiding is far more than a game. While children desperately need intimacy beginning in their earliest life moments, many don't experience it in the home or elsewhere. I know I didn't. Consider all the things every child must learn and experience regardless of how good or bad the home environment is. Consider the mistakes every child makes—the failures, inadequacies, and blunders—as well as the fear, anxiety, and simple uneasiness about how they are uniquely different from their peers.

Unfortunately, rather than gathering support and confidence from relationships with their parents, many children hide their inadequacies and failures, primarily out of fear of not being accepted. Children often learn to put on a false persona—one they think will be pleasing to others. Rather than reveal their true selves, they put on an act. Some never stop acting as they grow older. Intimacy can't flourish, or even take hold, when knowing yourself or the nature of the person you choose to be with isn't based in reality.

Now you know my working definition of *intimacy*, and you've seen a small glimpse of how intimacy benefits us. Hopefully, you feel you're not alone as you realize that all of us struggle to some extent with the areas that keep us from intimacy. You may be starting to understand some benefits of truly intimate relationships. But given all of that, what is holding you and so many other people back? Why did it take me almost twenty years of marriage to begin searching for intimacy, even though, in the early days of my recovery, I didn't know that was what was happening? We'll examine this in the next chapter and consider what might be holding us back.

NEXT STEP

Your next step for this chapter is to simply sit for a moment with my definition of *intimacy* and consider your most important relationships. Do you have certainty that each bulleted item is occurring regularly in the relationship? Which items call for something to change? Throughout the rest of the book, we'll examine how to make those changes happen.

CHAPTER 2

What's Holding Us Back?

Why did I wait so long? I pondered that one question the most in my earliest days of working on my intimacy problem. When I started experiencing real intimacy with others, it changed my life in so many wonderful ways that I was angry with myself for waiting so long. An important growth step for me was to forgive myself. I'll talk more about that process in a later chapter, but for now I bring it up because I needed to give myself grace and forgiveness with regard to my waiting. There were real things holding me back, and some of these same things may hold you and others back from truly becoming intimate with others.

I now realize that a primary thing holding many back from intimacy is fear. Please understand that fear is not a bad thing. Fear of being burned keeps us from putting our hand into a fire. The fear of being hit by a truck effectively deters us from stepping out into oncoming traffic on a busy street. Fear of hurting my beautiful bride again is no doubt playing a part today in helping me remain sexually pure and holy in our marriage. However, fear can also debilitate and keep humans from doing what they really need to do. For example, some may choose not to pursue a romantic relationship simply because they are afraid of being rejected. And many who are in relationships also fear rejection or abandonment, which keeps them from allowing their darkest secrets to be known.

It's also important to understand that fear isn't the only thing holding us back from intimacy. But it is, or can be, one of the most significant hindrances to our finding intimacy.

As we look at fear, you'll notice that much of this chapter ties directly to my story. I realize or hope that most of you reading this book didn't experience a past like mine. Because of this likely difference in our backgrounds, you may be tempted to question whether the things I'll note even apply to you. But even though our experiences may differ, I encourage you to consider that to varying degrees, most, if not all, of us share the fears I'm about to discuss. Also, keep in mind that according to an online article from the National Library of Medicine, "Approximately one-third of women and one-fifth of men will be victims of abuse." And, from the same article, "According to the CDC, . . . about 1 in 3 women and nearly 1 in 6 men experience some form of sexual violence during their lifetimes. Intimate partner violence, sexual violence, and stalking are high, with intimate partner violence occurring in over 10 million people each year."[4] These statistics don't even factor in how many people have never reported the abuse they suffered as children at the hands of a parent, teacher, coach, or loved one. There are many, many hurting people who likely can directly relate to various things I'll share. Like me, these hurting people have fears.

However, there are many fears we have regardless of whether we are victims of abuse. We're afraid we won't be understood. We fear we'll never succeed. Our fears, at times, appear to be endless. It's helpful to think about these and admit that they exist. Doing so was necessary for me to experience intimacy. For example, one fear that held me back was the fear of being hurt.

The Fear of Being Hurt

I've yet to meet a person who has not been hurt at least once in their life after choosing to be vulnerable. Sometimes, that hurt goes deep and is extremely painful. Because of this hurt and pain, wounded individuals may cut off a willingness to be open with others for fear of being hurt again. They live privately

---

[4] Martin Huecker et al., "Domestic Violence," National Library of Medicine, accessed June 19, 2024, https://www.ncbi.nlm.nih.gov/books/NBK499891/.

and guard their vulnerability closely. After all, it's reasonable not to want to be hurt again.

My fear of being hurt was another large stumbling block to intimacy in my life. I know I'm not alone. Many people live in fear of being hurt again because others have seriously hurt them in their past. This fear alone, if not properly addressed, may forever keep them from intimacy. For me, this fear stems from my childhood.

I was born in the early 1970s. Like most American children of the seventies, I was born into a typical two-parent household. Unfortunately, my parents divorced when I was four years old. Not long after the divorce, my mother remarried. As was commonplace, custody of children after divorce went to the mother, regardless of how fit or unfit she was.

All human beings have problems. None of us are perfect. However, some people have serious psychological problems. My mother was one of those. She carried those problems through her first marriage and right into her second marriage. It's common for victims of abuse to become abusive. This is true of my mother. It's also reasonably common for victims of abuse to marry abusers. This is, sadly, also true of my mother in her choice of her second husband.

The second man she married was verbally, emotionally, and physically abusive to her. This man, whom I would call "Dad" for the next fourteen years of my life, also abused me and my brother. One of my earliest childhood memories is of a loud argument (common for the home I lived in) that resulted in my mother being thrown through the screen door of our home. I remember crying and being afraid for my mother. I remember feeling afraid of what might then happen to me. *Fear* is probably the best word to describe my day-to-day state of mind as a child and adolescent. I learned to believe every person had to protect themselves from everyone else.

While I wish the abuse I experienced at the hands of my stepfather had been all I had to worry about as a child, it wasn't. As I've said, my mom was abusive as well. Just like my stepfather, she abused me verbally, emotionally, and physically. Additionally, as I have only recently been able to define it clearly, she abused me sexually. As I grew into my teen years, I also was a victim of rape by an older woman. All of this, along with the failure of my biological father and others to protect me, led me to fear everything and everyone. Ultimately, I trusted no one. I was afraid that even those closest to me, maybe especially those closest to me, would somehow hurt me.

The Fear of Facing Self

Another fear through many years of my life was the fear of facing myself and the responsibility I bore for my own shortcomings. I knew admitting I had been unfaithful to my wife in both thought and action would cause her immense hurt. Facing the reality that the amount of time and money I had spent on porn and other acting-out behavior had led to our being much farther behind financially than we might have been would rightfully lead to justified anger at me from my entire family. I wonder how many people know deep down that they are broken and have done terrible things in the past, but resist thinking about it because they know it will be painful. They pretend their past is not there, as I did, living and thinking as if the bad things had never happened. Rather than doing the hard work of facing reality and the tough parts of their past, seeking forgiveness, and making amends, they continue to live a life of hiding, often from both themselves and others.

When hiding exists, intimacy can never take place. Early in my recovery journey, I read a book by Donald Miller called *Scary Close*. It was instrumental in helping me understand myself and the hiding behavior ever-present in me. In *Scary Close*, Miller traces his personal life story about how his childhood started him down a path of falsehood and acting. Until close to the age of forty, he, like me, never fully experienced intimacy in a relationship with a woman because he wasn't able to stop acting.

One of the most touching things in the book is his account of a very personal moment of his childhood and how it forever affected his life.[5] Miller discusses how his inability to control his bladder affected him as a child. He recalls a specific day when he wet himself

---

[5]   Donald Miller, *Scary Close: Dropping the Act and Finding True Intimacy* (Nashville: Nelson Books, 2015), 25–27.

at school, tried desperately to cover it up, was caught, and was dreadfully embarrassed. I'm sure being a kid, Miller must have believed "no one else has ever had an issue like this." Isn't that the way we all think about our issues? No one's issues are like our own, or so we tell ourselves.

When I read Miller's story, I could relate immediately. Maybe you can too. There was no intimacy in that classroom. This is true even though Miller's teacher desired it. After he ran away, she chased him down and tried to be supportive of him. But his reaction was the same as my reaction for years to my own personal mess. I needed to hide. A story or a cover-up was required. I needed to act as though I was not who I really was, because if anyone knew I was really a guy who "peed my pants," so to speak, no one would love me. My response to difficult circumstances was to run and hide from the truth. I could never stop to look squarely at it and get help, love, and support to address my problems.

To take this matter a step further, Miller recounts what his actions were that day. First, he tried to cover up his bladder mishap and hide the issue. As he remarks, it was pretty silly and completely ineffective. Yet this was his first response. For many of us, trying to hide is our first response too. Second, Miller's embarrassment and covering up forced him to act further to protect his hiding. This meant wearing a coat in a warm classroom, trying desperately to keep the other kids from seeing his wet pants. Then, when the hiding failed, he blamed something else. And when all that fell apart, he experienced teasing and shaming from his classmates before running away.

Most people who engage in a process of hiding, avoidance, and running learn there are terrible consequences of doing so. This was the case for me. Here are some consequences of a life of hiding. First, hiders live a falsehood. As a result, those who routinely hide are always at war with themselves. They always, down deep, know their own reality. While we like to think otherwise, we all are pants pee-ers! Hiders simply can't face that reality.

The second consequence for hiders is that they don't allow themselves to put on a fresh pair of pants. They also don't get help to fix their pants-peeing problem. Rather, hiders search for ways to cover their stains and hide the stench. Worse yet, because of the embarrassment hiders have over their own issues, hiders usually become very good at pointing out others' problems. To divert the focus away from the huge stain on their wet pants, hiders are quick to point out the tiniest of marks on others' pants.

Finally, and most tragically, hiders experience the reality that they never can be deeply intimate with anyone. This robs them of life-giving support, which all humanity needs. Hiding keeps us from becoming the people we otherwise could be. It would be bad enough if our hiding only affected us, but our hiding significantly affects others, especially those who really care about us. Hiders don't allow others the ability to help them overcome. This robs others of the joy of being an intimate friend. I will always remember how sad my wife was when she learned that I had not felt I could stop hiding sooner because I did not trust her early in our relationship.

The Fear of Consequences

While I suffered horrible and inexcusable abuse as a child, that is not an excuse for the things I did. I'm responsible for each and every one of my own actions. By the age of twelve, I had become addicted to porn and sex. Sexual stimulation was my drug of choice. I used it whenever I was lonely or afraid. When I think back now, I realize how many women and others I hurt because of my addiction. I'll address it more later, but the use of pornography is an epidemic today in America and the world. The porn industry abuses women and children. Every dollar spent on pornography is hurting people, yet people spend billions every year on porn. I was a part of that. Besides supporting the abuse of women through the purchase of porn, I am also responsible for hurting many women because of the years I saw them as objects rather than humans created in the image of God.

Here's the thing. I knew all this nine years ago, as I know it today. I knew it while I was using my drug. But I was afraid of being honest about my addiction. I was afraid of facing and admitting my wrongs and the damage I caused. For more than forty years of my life, I pretended none of that had happened. I acted as if that wasn't me and I wasn't responsible. What would have happened if, back then, I had faced head-on the responsibility for my actions?

Few of us have lived lives in which we have not somehow hurt others, either knowingly or unknowingly. Many people have learned the importance of quickly acknowledging the wrongs they've done and seeking forgiveness. But, depending on just how broken our past is and how much damage we've caused, we may feel that both our past and the damage caused are unforgivable and that the consequences of that damage are insurmountable. The combined fear of facing the consequences of my wrongs and of my past becoming known probably kept me from intimacy for most of my life.

The fact is, I had so miserably failed in the sexual holiness of our marriage that I was scared I would lose everything if the truth ever came out. I feared losing my family. I love my kids, even if my actions as a husband and father haven't always shown that. Because of fear, my thoughts went like this: *My kids could never accept me if they knew the real me. They certainly couldn't or wouldn't respect me. In fact, they might just significantly rebel, and I would ruin their lives just like I've ruined mine.* These were serious fears to me. I allowed this fear of the consequences of my actions to keep me in hiding for far too long.

The Fear of Being Unforgivable

This fear of ourselves, of who we really are, and facing the consequences of our actions is real. So is the fear of being unforgivable. Many of us hold a deep fear that we are unforgivable. I never believed I could be forgiven for many of the things I had done in my past. I mean, how can a wife forgive an unfaithful husband? It just didn't seem possible. I believed that the dark, scary truths and ugliness within me were just too much. It would require too much grace, mercy, and forgiveness. I'm not sure about you, but I'm not nearly as gracious, merciful, or forgiving as I should be with others, or with myself. Giving grace, extending mercy, and being willing to forgive is difficult. It takes effort and desire. It goes against everything in our human nature, our selfish side, which says we don't have to give grace and forgiveness.

For the past nine years of my life, I've been involved in a wonderful organization called FirstLight. FirstLight exists to help men and women trapped in the consequences of sexual dysfunction. Our world desperately needs many more organizations doing such work, as well as volunteers. Initially, I got to know FirstLight as a broken man in need of help. My counselor strongly recommended I join a group to find support and help in a community of others. I found that help and will forever be grateful to those who were a part of my recovery. This includes my personal counselor, our marriage counselor, and the many individuals who supported my wife as we worked through my brokenness.

Alongside a lot of work to restore my marriage relationship and truly become intimate with my wife and others, I began taking part in a weekly FirstLight small group where men experienced the freedom of intimate connection with other guys. The men in FirstLight groups have a safe space where they can be known without judgment. Many of these men enter FirstLight feeling alone and trapped, and believing there is no way out of their struggles with porn and other sex-related problems, including sexual addiction. However, one of the greatest things these men experience in the group is forgiveness. I'll never forget the day when, after about six months of meetings, my group leader said, "Rob, it sounds like maybe you are starting to forgive yourself." I think he said this because in place of being very critical and hard on myself for the mess I had made of my life, I began to give myself some grace. I began seeing myself as someone who is lovable. My group leader was right. I was finally forgiving myself.

Understand, this realization occurred only after six months of forgiveness and acceptance by other men in that circle. From my first night in group, I met unconditional acceptance. No matter what I shared about myself and my past, others accepted me. I didn't feel judged. I felt forgiven. While it's hard for me to even get my head around it, there were a number of things that ultimately led to my coming to a place where I could forgive myself. Yes, experiencing the forgiveness of others was a big part of that process. But so, too, was my beginning to *seek* true forgiveness from others. Maybe it was because I chose to do all I could, all that was in my power, to genuinely confess and make things right. Maybe it was because when I put in that effort, others simply allowed me to do so. Whatever the case, all of this played a part in bringing me to a place where I could forgive myself. Every part also helped move me past my fear that I was unforgivable. I sometimes wonder how many people will never receive forgiveness because they simply believe they are unforgivable.

The Fear of Hurting Others

Closely related to the fears just discussed is the fear of hurting others. Believe it or not, I really care about people. A few years back, after reading a book by Simon Sinek called *Start with Why*,[6] I focused my insurance career on helping people know why they should work with me. Why do I exist? What drives me? What is my mission? The core response to these questions is: I exist to help others. That's the opposite of hurting others. Because of this drive, I have a reasonable fear of hurting other people. But it's not simply my drive to help others that leads to this fear.

Sadly, most of my fear of hurting others comes from my abusive upbringing. I wrongly believed I did not deserve help if getting that help might bring hurt to others. As a child, if I cried because of the terribleness of any situation at home, I would be hit or shaken hard. To avoid that, I would not cry out for help. I couldn't simply say, "I'm scared." The main reason for keeping it locked inside was because my mother's happiness or state of mind was often determined by me. She

---

[6]   Simon Sinek, *Start with Why: How Great Leaders Inspire Everyone to Take Action* (New York: Portfolio, 2009).

frequently told me this. If I dared to talk about my own issues or problems, it caused problems or issues for her. I couldn't bear the emotional barrage I would face as she shared how much hurt and pain she experienced because of my actions.

Basically, through this dysfunctional cycle, I learned to feel responsible for the emotional and physical well-being of others. If I was good, there was a better chance Mom would be happy. Being pleasing to her was important because it made life overall better for me. She was always willing to share how terrible her life was, and as a result, I felt even more terrible about my own. My problems, my hurts, my fears did not compare with hers or certainly weren't as important as hers. This is what I believed growing up.

I did not realize until I worked closely with a counselor how damaging that was to me. It wounded me. It also deeply confused me. Plus, it helped facilitate and strengthen a disastrous shame cycle. See, I hurt people, as all of us do from time to time, because we are not perfect. We make mistakes, and often mistakes hurt people. But, according to the twisted code I formed in childhood, I believed I shouldn't hurt people no matter what, especially the people closest to me. I thought that as a human being, I was a complete failure. This was part of a cycle of thinking I lived with for most of my life. Ultimately, this cycle, and specifically my fear of hurting others, facilitated much of my lying and hiding. It killed any chance of intimacy.

The Fear That Others Will Fail Us

I wish those were the only fears that kept me from intimacy. They alone were enough. But there were two other main fears I faced. These final two are ones you may face as well. The first is that I had a genuine fear that others would fail me. I've already discussed being hurt by others. Being failed by others is different. It relates more to trust. Intimacy requires trust, as we'll discuss in some depth in future chapters. I have a tough time trusting others because of how others—primarily my family—failed me.

In much the same way as the other fears stemmed from my upbringing, the fear of being failed by others most certainly did. My parents failed me on a regular basis. I couldn't trust them. For example, I was used as a human pawn in arguments over finances with my biological father. Both my mother and stepfather manipulated others and asked me to say things or do things contrary to the truth, simply to benefit themselves. A major betrayal that had an impact on me in many ways happened when I was a senior in high school. My mother left my brother and me with my abusive stepfather while she flew to Las Vegas with her new boyfriend, blowing my college savings fund in the process.

Through all of this, I learned early on that I could not depend on others. Rather, I had to depend on myself for everything I needed. I had to develop some sense of what is true or not true. I had to find some means of enjoying life. I had to find some way to provide for my future, with no guidance. This was a recipe for disaster. I think many people who have experienced severe loss or hurt by close family members question who they can trust. Many subconsciously determine that no one is trustworthy. Therefore, they learn to lean solely on themselves rather than opening up to pursue intimacy.

Others learn to find something else to depend on, which can be any number of things. Often, that something else becomes an addiction, because it is so needed for coping with life. For some, the addiction is to a physical substance that must be acquired and regularly consumed in some way, but other addictions require only the individual and can fit into the mold of self-reliance. For instance, some people learn to depend on alcohol to numb the pain and difficulty of life's challenges. For others, food becomes their solace. For still others, it is illicit drugs. For me, it was porn and sexual acting out. Since I couldn't depend on others because they would surely fail me, I needed something I could depend on. Fantasy resided in my mind and required nothing other than me. Plus, it could quickly remove me from my present circumstances, whatever those might be. So, for me, sexual release became my substitute for healthy relationships with others.

The Fear of Losing One's Intimacy Substitute

Because that was my life for so long, I unknowingly at the time had another fear—fear of losing my life coping strategy. Many who are failing in their intimate relationships have something they are using to replace that need. They likely don't want to admit it, but it would be quite scary to them to give that "thing" up. Sometimes, even harmful things can become our closest friend. The alcoholic, if she's honest, needs to face the fact that she must completely stop drinking. The drug addict needs to determine that there won't be another high to escape to when he's suffering the actual pains of life. For those who are grappling with addictions of any stripe, the fear of losing whatever we are addicted to is real.

In the early days of recovery from my porn addiction, a direct question was posed to me: "Do you want to get well?" Sounds like a stupid question, doesn't it? Who doesn't want to get well? When the question was asked, though, I was encouraged not to respond too quickly. Rather, I was encouraged to think about all the reasons I shouldn't get well. It sounds counterintuitive, but it's not. Every addict needs to seriously think about what it's going to cost and what they are going to have to give up if they stand any chance at long-term sobriety. See, there were reasons for my porn use. While my need for it sickened me and caused terrible intimacy issues, the highs from the sexual stimulation were great. There are reasons addicts begin using in the first place and reasons they keep using.

Ultimately, facing my fear of losing my vice head-on was important. It was crucial to me to be able to honestly say, "I fear not having that immediate high whenever I want it. I fear facing life without it." When others understood and supported me, rather than judging or condemning me, it helped me overcome this fear. It's tragically unfortunate that it took me more than forty years of living to give up my coping solution. But if I had to list one reason over any other why it took so long, it would probably be this: Though I wanted to be well, I simply did not want it enough to do what it would take to be well. I was too afraid of all the consequences that would naturally occur. It just appeared to be too great a risk, so I stayed shackled in my addiction.

You may read this and not currently be dealing with any form of addiction. I hope that's the case. However, let me ask you a few questions, and I ask you to be brutally honest with yourself. Is there anything in your life you would not give up for the sake of intimacy? Is fear holding you back in any way? What is it you are afraid of? At this point in your understanding of intimacy and what is required to achieve it, you might say no. There often are things that hold us back, and sometimes we are simply not willing to let those things go. Still, as you continue to grow and learn, I encourage you to revisit these questions.

The Fear of Being Known

If none of the fears I've shared have resonated with you, let me share one I know we all struggle with. In my mind, it is the biggest stumbling block to relationships becoming intimate. That fear is the fear of being known.

I can assure you we are all guilty in some ways of living falsely and are scared to death of really being known. We're fearful of what others think, of how they perceive us. Again, in *Scary Close*, Miller shares a story about a man he met who sustained a very serious head injury as an adult. One outcome of the injury was that "he became uncomfortably blunt."[7] Miller points out that the man had no desire to be rude or hurtful, but he seemed unrestricted in what he said, the way he dressed, and how he approached others. It was remarkable to Miller because it was so strange.

Reading the story, I couldn't help but realize what a condemnation that is on all of us. I have met no one like that. I have certainly been nothing like that. Every person I have ever met has been, like me, guarded, at least to a certain degree. We learn it at a very early age. We're sucked in by advertising and the simple ebb and flow of cultural mores. The result of this is often a lack of satisfaction with and a careful preservation of our real selves. We hide the truth about what we feel and what we want—usually out of fear of being known. The result is a loss of intimacy. How well do you allow others to really know you? As we'll discuss in the next chapter, the answer to that question likely determines the extent to which you are experiencing intimacy now.

---

[7]   Miller, *Scary Close*, 144–45.

NEXT STEP

This chapter poses a lot of deep questions. Hopefully, you thought through them. My encouragement to you right now is to do two things. First, give yourself grace. That doesn't mean continue in destructive patterns and avoid facing the consequences of the harm you've caused. Instead, believe you can be different. Second, if you're trying to get better (with intimacy or anything else), stop going it alone. This may mean calling a professional therapist for help or simply asking a friend to lovingly support and encourage you as you seek to become a better person. Tell them what you're doing and why, and invite them to join you. This is tackling fear head-on.

CHAPTER 3

The Necessity of Being Known

As I just shared, fear of being known kept me from experiencing intimacy for far too long. Worry about rejection, abandonment, and embarrassment are debilitating. I wish I could say that none of those things hinder me today and I'm always open to fully being known. But that would be a bold lie. Being known itself is hard. Deciding to even be willing to be known can be even harder. One thing I now understand from being in several intimate relationships with others is that it really is a choice. It's a decision that we make. Either we open ourselves up to being known or we don't.

For me, a big part of being known started not with others, but with getting to know myself. I recognized that in order for others to know me, three things were required. First, I had to know me. Next, I needed to allow what I learned to be shared. Finally, another person would have to receive who I am as I am. I don't think we often break the steps out like this, but that doesn't mean they don't follow like this.

Sadly, there are many people caught where I once was. They are not only unknown to others but also truly not known by themselves. What is potentially even sadder is that some of these people will never get the professional help they need to become known. Many of the fears I shared in the previous chapter came to light through weekly counseling sessions with my therapist. There were journaling exercises I went through, books I read, and lots of open, honest sharing with others. It was hard work!

I didn't like me. It was painful to admit the truth about who I was and what I had become to myself, much less to others. In some strange way, I thought I could get through life without thinking about the real me. I realize now some of this was an attempt to protect myself from the terrible truths of lived life experiences. Memories of past traumatic events and feelings lived inside me that I couldn't share even with myself. I couldn't honestly face these things for a long time. In fact, I'm quite certain there are some things my mind still won't let me face. That might sound weird to you, but it's true. Those who have experienced abuse and/or extreme trauma often cannot be real with themselves. As a safety mechanism, our minds can repress significant parts of our past. We psychologically (either consciously or unconsciously) choose not to think about things that are overwhelmingly painful.

In fact, while I was writing this book, a friend of mine was diagnosed with "transient global amnesia." My friend was in a Bible study group at church and began telling her personal faith testimony. From all she can recall, and all that those around her recall, as she was sharing, she mentally connected with traumatic experiences she'd had growing up. This reexposure to those memories resulted in a temporary episode of memory loss. Trauma affects people physically as well as emotionally. Post-traumatic stress disorder (PTSD) is real and affects many individuals of every ethnicity, race, creed, sex, or any other way we may try to differentiate people. According to the National Institute of Mental Health, "Anyone can develop PTSD at any age. This includes combat veterans and people who have experienced or witnessed a physical or sexual assault, abuse, an accident, a disaster, or other serious events. . . . According to the National Center for PTSD, a program of the U.S. Department of Veterans Affairs, about six out of every 100 people will experience PTSD at some point in their lives."[8] Consider that—those numbers, as high as they are, are based on confirmed cases. How many have PTSD but will never be diagnosed?

---

[8]   "Post-Traumatic Stress Disorder," National Institute of Mental Health, May 2024, accessed June 19, 2024, https://www.nimh.nih.gov/health/topics/post-traumatic-stress-disorder-ptsd.

Unfortunately, the conditions I've described are far more common than one might think. So many people in our society carry deep scars that continue to wound them throughout their lives. Whether a person's unconscious mind has barricaded the overwhelming pain in a vault too deep to be reached, or the individual has consciously buried the experiences away, thinking that will prevent the memories from causing harm, those experiences have altered and will continue to alter that person's life. Many who have experienced trauma have never revealed their wounds to another human being, including a trained counselor who might be able to help them process their hurt.

Ultimately, whether they realize it or not, people who are intentionally walling off their trauma are deceiving not only others but themselves. They carry themselves in such a way as to say, "Look at me, I'm fine. I have it all together," when in fact they are hanging on by a thread, hoping something or someone doesn't trigger a memory, hurt, or feeling that would wreck them. Donald Miller nails this when he says, "deception in any form kills intimacy."[9] If we are walking around in a way that translates as "everything is fine" when it's not, we are practicing deception and inhibiting intimacy. When we deceive others like this, what we are really saying is that we are unwilling to be known. Often, we deceive ourselves as much as we deceive others.

---

[9]   Miller, *Scary Close*, 103. Miller credits authors Henry Cloud and John Townsend as his source for this idea: "One of the things Henry Cloud and John Townsend convinced me of in *Safe People* is that deception in any form kills intimacy."

Thinking about this and the process I went through in being known, I'm amazed at the extent to which I had lied to myself for years. My process basically went like this. I was asked direct questions like "What are the things you've done that you're most embarrassed about?" "What are your primary character defects?" and "In what areas of life do you recognize you have little to no control?" Then I honestly journaled answers to those questions. Something interesting happens when you write something down, and I can still remember the discomfort I felt as I wrote things about myself that I hadn't openly revealed before in my life. The next step was to share those things with my counselor, my group members, and, ultimately, my wife.

But it all started with being real with myself. For me, intimacy began with knowing Rob authentically. This also meant admitting, "Yes, this is who I am. Yes, this is what I believe." It also meant facing the reality that I have serious character defects. One of my major character defects is pride. If it weren't so sad, it would be funny that even in writing the sentence "I have serious character defects," I wanted to change "have" to "had" to sound better about myself. It might be humorous for you to know that my editor and I had a laugh at what I just wrote because she initially wanted to change my "have" to "had" also! Knowing myself required me to face head-on who I am, acknowledging the good, the bad, and the ugly. Before I could share with others that pride is one of my character defects, I had to share and accept in myself that pride is a character defect I struggle with. Yes, I'm getting better with it. But I'm convinced it will be a lifelong battle that I'll need to win minute by minute and day by day.

One of the more challenging understandings about myself came from an internal conflict I struggled with for years. Despite years in the church as a church leader and years in the pulpit as an ordained pastor, I had significant questions about God. And it's not only that I had questions about God. In some ways, I was furious with God. I remember the first time I wrote that down in my journal. I thought lightning was going to strike me. It felt weird to put a thought like that down on paper. It's interesting to think about why I couldn't share something like that. I believe it's primarily because of the reverence I hold for God and the fact that I know God is ultimately perfect in what He does. But it's possible I had other reasons, like fear of upsetting or offending God. Remember, while this was me, I had been hiding myself from myself for many years. I can still remember telling my counselor about this, and I remember his response: "Do you think that surprises God?" It made me chuckle then, and it makes me chuckle now.

Why is this important? Throughout my life, from those who educated me to things I read and learned, I believed several things about God. Yet my personal experiences periodically butted up against some of these beliefs. This left me confused, angry, and depressed. However, because it's God we're talking about, and God is true and never wrong, could I be honest about that confusion, anger, and depression? I didn't think so back then. I now know otherwise.

For example, from my grandmother and every church I attended, I heard repeatedly that "God loves you."

If you have spent any time as a child in church, you probably can sing the children's hymn "Jesus Loves Me" right along with me:

> Jesus loves me! This I know,
> For the Bible tells me so.
> Little ones to Him belong;
> They are weak, but He is strong.
>
> Yes, Jesus loves me!
> Yes, Jesus loves me!
> Yes, Jesus loves me!
> The Bible tells me so.

Before going further, I will say I absolutely believe this to be true! There's no doubt in my mind. After all, Jesus died on a cross to pay the penalty for my sin because of His great love for me.

And yet . . . if God really loves me, why did He allow me to suffer all the abuse I went through? How does that show love? I'm confused. If God is all powerful and has everything under control, then please tell me why there couldn't have been a better plan? Worse, how do I reconcile my significant anger about my past, really believing God allowed that past, with the proper appreciation and thankfulness I absolutely should have for my salvation?

Knowing myself meant coming to terms with all this. Accepting myself for who I am and feeling fine saying, "It's okay that I don't have it all together. I don't have to have it all together. In fact, I'll never have it all together!" was significant growth for me. It was the sign that significant healing had taken place. For the longest time, it was hard to believe that it was perfectly acceptable to be broken and not have everything together. Growing up, I was made to believe I should be perfect. Let me tell you plainly, I'll never be perfect. Neither will you. There is a profound sense of freedom, understanding, and healing that happens when we can not only say things like that but honestly believe them to be true.

Once I got to that point—and it took a long time to get to that point—only then could I tackle the next stage of being known. Sharing the true me with others proved to be tough. I discovered it's one thing to know and accept yourself and a totally different thing to reveal that person to others. I had grown so accustomed to wearing a mask for so many years that I didn't even know how not to wear one.

As I thought about the possibility of sharing the real me with others, I had to face two troublesome questions: How much of me and my story should I share? And how much do I need to share? I found that the correct answers were not so simple. Reaching them required answering a few other questions: How much intimacy do I want in the relationship? Is this relationship going to be defined by intimacy? Can I trust the person I am considering opening myself up to?

My goal is to have intimate, authentic relationships with everyone. This is not possible in the blink of an eye, although it is possible to make most of my relationships gradually more intimate. To the extent that it relies on me, I want as much intimacy as possible with those I care about. At an absolute minimum, I decided early in my journey that I needed intimacy with my wife. I wanted our marriage to be defined by intimacy. So how much of me and my story did I need to tell her? All of it.

Before I share more, I want to confess, I know that many of us hide way more of our stories than we would like to admit. Let me ask you to consider a couple of questions. What is your deepest, darkest secret? You know, the secret about you and your life that reveals the terribleness inside you? Or, possibly your deepest, darkest secret is about the hurt you've experienced—hurt that, to this day, brings immense feelings of pain, anger, or sadness. Maybe it's the type of secret that, if revealed, could hurt another person, possibly the person you care most about? Second question: Have you shared this deep secret, or any of your lesser ones, for that matter, with any other human being?

In addiction circles, it's common to talk about the "last 10 percent." Most addicts will share about 90 percent of their story. But the actual work of recovery truly begins with being open and honest about the remaining 10 percent. Most addicts, and frankly most people, resist sharing the last 10 percent, which includes the ugliest parts of themselves. But it's in sharing that last 10 percent and finding acceptance after doing so that we really find intimacy. That intimacy occurs because the secrets are gone. There is freedom to be who we are. It's a truly amazing feeling to be accepted and loved as our real selves—not the selves we wish we were. Once I realized that, the desire to share more of myself with others who truly cared about me became much more natural.

Even when we're making progress, though, mistakes and missteps fill the early days of living with an intention to be known. For example, I was mistaken in believing that everyone wants relationships marked by intimacy and, therefore, everyone naturally wanted to know me. Sometimes, especially in the early days of recovery, I overshared with people who didn't want to go that deep. Typically, I'd then experience their rejection. I still struggle with this mistake sometimes. This rejection caused further hurt and made me question whom I could trust. Jesus provided His followers some great advice in Matthew 7:6: "Do not give dogs what is holy, and do not throw your pearls before pigs, lest they trample them underfoot and turn to attack you."

I now understand some important truths that relate directly to what Jesus instructed. First, like pearls, my story is precious. Who I am is valuable. With all my character defects and all my problems, I am a human who is worth loving and worth knowing. But I do live in a world with a lot of dogs and pigs! It's wise to consider the spirit of others and seek to determine whether they really are a pig before "throwing my pearls" before them. I like the term "safe people," which one of my counselors shared with me. It often takes time to determine who is and who is not a safe person. Safe people are those who have demonstrated over time that they can be trusted. Safe people demonstrate that they not only care about us but can, with compassion, hear us and refrain from inappropriate judgment. Obviously, those who are safe do not gossip and will protect privileged information we share.

Also, it's important to be aware that just because someone should be a safe person doesn't automatically make them so. For example, many church leaders, including pastors, are not safe. While church leaders should be understanding, empathetic, and able to retain the confidence of those they communicate with, sometimes they are not. Sometimes they don't have the right training to really be the help that they might want to be. Worse, some can do more damage than good by their inappropriate responses to the hurt of others. That's unfortunate but true. In addition, many pastors have their own deep hurts and struggles in their own stories but don't get the help they need—and often feel they have no one in their pastoral circles to turn to.

However, the overwhelming majority of professional counselors and therapists are safe. This is only one of many reasons why I believe most people need such professional counselors and therapists at some point in their lives. These professionals are bound by their licensing and our legal environment to be safe. They serve an important role in the lives of many simply because they can be trusted to be safe people.

While the world is full of pigs and those who are not safe, I learned that it's not only professional counselors and therapists who are safe. Others who don't have a degree in psychotherapy really can be trusted. It's those safe people I can trust who have the privilege of hearing and receiving me and my story. Initially, it took me a long time to believe anyone could be trusted. This time period was lengthened because of the pigs I came across. Because of this, I had to learn an appropriate balance between living with the desire to be known and sharing only when it made sense. Initially, it was only my wife, my counselor, and the men in my FirstLight recovery group who received my pearls. These people shared their pearls with me as well. Over time, though, I found others who were trustworthy and could be safely trusted with significant parts of my story so that they might come to fully know me.

Please understand, I've still made, and I still make, mistakes in my judgment. There are people I really wanted not to be dogs and pigs, but they turned out to be. It's also worth noting that many people are at different places in their lives in terms of their ability to accept another's stories. Let's face reality. Most people live in shallow relationships. There are things we don't allow others into. In most relationships, our deepest feelings and worst habits remain hidden. Areas of secrecy commonly exist that we think are "sacred cows" not to be talked about. There are some thoughts, feelings, and life experiences we don't touch. For some, hidden family relationships are untouchable. For others, it's past friendships they'd rather not think about, much less talk about. Others hold their upbringing, values, and experiences as sacred and private. Because folks like this have no intention of sharing their own brokenness and wrongly believe we shouldn't share our brokenness, they may simply not be able to receive our pearls.

For me, the biggest change in being known started at home. Because I had hidden so much from my wife and lied habitually throughout many years of marriage, regaining trust and being known were *the* primary goals if my marriage was going to last. I could no longer secretly live two lives. I had to be known. Living as a fraud was no longer acceptable. It was imperative that I bring all of what I was hiding inside me into the light. Honesty in all areas of life was the new me. My wife had to know the person she really was married to. I decided I would no longer hide anything from her. I would make myself open to her regardless of how much it would hurt me or her. Further, and because I needed it, I set up boundaries and requirements that would force me to share.

For example, I decided early in recovery I would never again go to a bar alone without telling my wife and getting her permission beforehand. Because bars had been a stumbling block for me in the past, this simply made sense. Craigslist was another boundary I set. My wife and I have used Craigslist for wholesome purposes quite a few times over the years. We've bought things from others, and my wife has sold pieces of furniture through listings. However, because I had abused the personals section of Craigslist for self-gratification, I set a hard rule. I would never again go on Craigslist without first telling Tammy why.

I literally have involved my wife in almost every aspect of my life. This is simply a safe place for both of us. For me, there is comfort in knowing that nothing I do, no place I go, is not known. For her, she appreciates knowing I am never going to hide anything from her ever again. If I'm known in small, benign things, she can count on me to be known in bigger things. Becoming seen and understood for my true self became a priority in my life. I sought to be known as much as I could be known. I wanted Tammy to know what I thought about. My feelings are important, and Tammy deserves to know them. If I fail as a human being, Tammy should know. Being known in every way possible was a brand-new reality for me that began nine years ago. It has made our relationship radically different from any other relationship I have ever been in, and radically wonderful.

It wasn't just my relationship with my wife that changed. As I realized the necessity of being completely known in my marriage, I remembered a primary metaphor used for God's relationship with His people. For Christians, the Bible defines this relationship as a "marriage." God is the groom, and His people (Christians) are the bride. I find it fascinating that the Bible uses "knowing" as the essential prerequisite for this marriage relationship. Consider the very profound statement that Jesus Christ made in Matthew 7:23 when talking about the people who ultimately would not be in heaven. He said, "And then will I declare to them, 'I never *knew* you; depart from me, you workers of lawlessness'" (italics mine).

There are several things that are simply staggering if we sincerely believe what Jesus said. First, it's troubling to think that Jesus uttered those words about people who likely think they are already in a marriage relationship with Him. Matthew 7:22 gives context for Jesus's radical statement. The people Jesus is talking about would be great people who had done amazing things based on a supposed relationship with Jesus. Some had even cast out demons in His name. Yet Jesus declared that despite what these people had claimed or what they had done, He "never knew" them. Understand, this may have even included some he was speaking with that day who would go on to do amazing things. Some of those people probably even talked face-to-face with Jesus. I'm betting many people like that then and now, basing their supposed marriage with Jesus on things they are doing out of whatever concept of Him they have, surely think they are going to heaven.

But take a moment and think about the truth of what Christ said. It really is a radical statement. Jesus said there were many who would *claim* to be in a relationship with Him. In verse 22, He declared, "many will say to me." I'm sure that among His audience that day, there were some who actively told others about the close relationship with God they thought they had. Some of them may have even publicly professed that they were right with God because they had participated in a public ceremony, such as baptism, declaring their faith. And yet Jesus claimed that a good number of these people weren't in the relationship they believed they were in. Despite what they said and despite what they'd done, these people were not in an intimate, knowing relationship with Jesus. They had never up and said, "God, I want You to know me for all that I am, and I want to know You as much as I can; and I'll give or do anything for it."

Continuing this line of thought, Jesus, being fully God, knows everyone. He knows everything about everyone. In fact, we can infer from Luke 12:7 that God even knows how many hairs you and I have on our heads—and, no doubt, why I don't have as many of them today as I once did. So, how is it that Jesus here declares, "I never knew you"? The problem is clearly not with Jesus. The problem is that many of His followers are not willing to be known, even to God.

Nine years ago, I realized I had been for many years in a relationship with God that was much like my relationship with my wife. God and I were spiritually married. I had a testimony and baptism to affirm that marriage with God, much like I had a ceremony and wedding ring to prove I was married to Tammy. But Tammy never knew me because I was not willing to be fully known. In much the same way, although God knew everything about me, I wasn't willing to be completely open with God about myself. God knew I was angry with Him, but something transformative happened in our relationship when I opened up to God about how I really felt. When I acknowledged my feelings and discussed them with Him, I became known. The more honest I was with God about who I was, how I felt, what

I believed, what I questioned, and where my concerns lay, the more God showed His love to me, letting me feel in my soul how much He had always known me and loved me even with all those internal feelings, beliefs, questions, and concerns.

Before moving on, let me reemphasize that the problem started with me. The core problem for many struggling with intimacy is themselves. It's tragic how many marriages are not what they could be because one partner refuses to be known. I'm convinced that the story Jesus told was not only about people who claimed to be in a marriage with God and weren't. That, by far, is most important and needs to be dealt with. But the story Jesus told also applies to many men and women in so-called marriage relationships.

I wonder how many of these couples in truth have a marriage at all. They tell others they're married, and a large number of them wear wedding bands showing the world they are united as one. Virtually all married couples have had a marriage ceremony wherein they exchanged vows and were pronounced "husband and wife." These couples even have government-issued documents stating that they're married. But despite all that, some husbands and wives do not know the deep truth about each other.

I believe that a significant percentage of married people don't know their spouse. I mean really know. They may know a lot about their spouse. They may even do all the things married people do. But they have never each independently made themselves fully known to each other. Often, this is due to one member being unwilling to be known. For some married couples, a friend outside the marriage may know more about what makes the individual who they are than their spouse does. It is a sad reality today that some men and women are living together, and possibly having sex together, but honestly are not much more than roommates pooling resources to make life a little easier for both. The idea of knowing each other, really knowing each other, is as foreign as speaking a language that neither has exposure to.

Tragically, living in a relationship like this leaves both parties missing the intimacy God intends for all in marital relationships. What's even sadder is that, many times, the person who is not willing to be known certainly could be. Not only that, but his or her spouse would also love and accept them. This is what I found to be true in my life. My wife wanted to love me. She wanted to know me and my inmost being, but I wouldn't let her do so for more than twenty years. It hurts me more than you can imagine when I consider how much pain I caused her by my unwillingness to allow myself to be known. This is especially true now, knowing that all that time, she was willing to know me, love me, and forgive me. My unwillingness to be known deprived both my wife and me of intimacy.

When I finally allowed myself to be known, I could not have foretold all the good that would come of it. I did not know how important it was to me in every area of my life. I had no knowledge that my hiding had been keeping me from the intimacy I desperately craved. Living in the light, with every area of myself exposed to God and to trusted others, was freeing. It allowed me, for the first time in my life, to be the husband and father I had always wanted to be. I began to genuinely connect with others. All the other important necessities for intimacy fell in line once I began letting myself be seen for exactly who I am. All the principles of developing and maintaining intimacy ultimately depend on whether we will know others and be known to others. This step simply is the greatest necessity.

NEXT STEP

How do you eat an elephant? One bite at a time. Depending on where you are in your intimacy journey, you may need to seek professional help to explore and share the deepest, most hidden parts of yourself. But can you start smaller today? The next step after reading this chapter is to quickly look at each of your most important relationships and decide this week to share one thing about yourself that the other person doesn't know. For example, consider your primary or even secondary character defects. Could you tell one of your closest loved ones that you have always struggled with "being judgmental of others" and are actively working on it? (If that one doesn't apply, just replace it with one of your actual shortcomings.) Ask if they might help hold you accountable as you work to improve in this area. It can be a small thing, but start the process.

CHAPTER 4

What's Truth Got to Do with It?

In the middle of my adolescence, Tina Turner released "What's Love Got to Do with It."[10] This song would become her only United States number one hit. As I write this in 2024, *Rolling Stone* magazine lists the song as number 134 on its list of "The 500 Greatest Songs of All Time."[11] For perspective, that's one slot above the Beatles hit "She Loves You." While I could question the voters' mental state when it comes to this placement, I am only going to comment on the fact that Turner's song is considered "great." In fact, over the

---

[10]   Tina Turner, "What's Love Got to Do with It," *Private Dancer* (Hollywood, CA: Capitol Records, 1984).

[11]   "The 500 Greatest Songs of All Time," *Rolling Stone*, February 16, 2024, https://www.rollingstone.com/music/music-lists/best-songs-of-all-time-1224767/.

years, it has climbed higher in that very same ranking. Why? The song essentially highlights the physical aspect of our sexuality. It promotes the basic idea that, at the heart of things, we're essentially beings primarily affected by visual and physical stimuli.

While the tune is catchy and Tina Turner had a dynamic voice, I can't help but wonder if one reason the song has been so successful is because it correctly captures the point of view to which many in America have resolved themselves. Because love is painful, why love? Since choosing to love often results in hurt and brokenness, isn't it better to be satisfied with the physical aspect of sexual relationships? That's the part that everyone enjoys and that, with no investment, doesn't cause any pain. After all, over the past thirty to forty years, Americans have practiced the theory that love is not essential to relationships—at least not love defined by honesty, transparency, and intimacy. In my opinion, the consequences have been devastating.

In 2024 America, the biblical concept of love is as old-fashioned as much of the music of a century ago. In some regards, love that requires effort, sacrifice, honesty, and commitment is so outdated, most of society has forgotten what older generations either normally practiced or at least understood to be true. Today, love is frequently believed to be one of two ideas, both of which are a far cry from the intimate love that society desperately needs.

The first harmful idea of love is that love is essentially a strong feeling of desire and want. Many people today mistakenly believe this. This love becomes a burning desire within them. Because sex or sexual stimuli usually fuel this desire, the desire itself can lead to addiction. It is essentially a burning passion that is quenched only by being with the object of that passion. I use the word *object* rather than *person* because often that is all the other person is—an object to satisfy a significant desire. This type of love is not much more than the love a passionate music lover has for their favorite band—a longing that's satisfied only by hearing the song they want through their speakers or earbuds.

Often, people who hold this view of love are quite content with staying in a relationship as long as the "feeling" is there. The "feeling" is really a personal satisfaction that stems from personally getting what they want out of the relationship. I'm not shocked at all today when I find out someone has abandoned what seemed to be a close relationship because they "fell out of love" or they seemingly overnight started "loving" someone totally different. With this prevalent mindset, it's not surprising that marriage is poorly regarded and many couples are content with simply living together rather than tying the knot. Because so many of these relationships are based more on sexual attraction than on truth, it's no wonder they don't stand the test of time.

Another equally troublesome and incorrect view of love has emerged that deviates from a central aspect of the love our hearts are really longing and crying for. This version of love seeks to find our ultimate fulfillment in another person. It's the idea of finding someone who "completes" or "fulfills" us; someone who will make us whole. The problem, though, is that it is impossible for any other human being to do that. Many people pour themselves heart, mind, and body into another person, expecting that person to produce the joy, excitement, and any number of other positive desires we have. Sometimes those desires seem to be met in and through the relationship. But they can never fully be met in another person. Because of how much is given into these relationships and how much is expected from them, as Tina Turner's song suggests, hearts often do get broken.

Many people, committed to this mistaken view of love, expect the other person to fill the holes in their heart, which, in reality, no human being can fill. For as long as I can remember, the concept "he or she completes me" has been seen as practically synonymous with love. Movies have portrayed this as the norm—that if I find the right person, my love partner will complete me as the perfect match, the yin to my yang. But as appealing as it seems, this is an illusion. We fail to face the truth. No other human being on this earth will ever be able to complete you. If you are not complete *without* someone else, you will never be complete *with* someone else. I believe many people, whether or not they're in a romantic relationship, are not complete in and of themselves.

In both incorrect views of love, there are a couple of troublesome undercurrents. First, and most important, both views of love are focused on how individuals can get what they want. Both are about meeting personal desires. Consequently, many people focus their attention on finding what they think or believe will do that. Their desire in both cases is so strong that they often don't do the hard work of digging in to know the other person. Sometimes, they may not even want to truly know the other person, because that might cloud their willingness to pursue them further.

Worse, men and women alike have a general idea of what others are looking for in a romantic partnership and what we think is needed to gain entry into a serious relationship. So, we're naturally inclined to promote our best selves and hide those things that could prevent us from being desired. Often, we don't do the hard work of finding out who others really are at their core. We don't get to the truth. Maybe we can't handle the truth? But ultimately, truth has everything to do with real love, and truth has everything to do with finding intimacy.

In my mind, the worst reality stemming from the wrong ideas of love is this: We are in love with counterfeits. This has colored our society as we have misunderstood, misrepresented, or simply ignored the truth. We have believed a lie. We've believed that truth is dangerous and we can't be truthful. To take this a step further, sometimes we are living a lie. Many of us learned in our youth to be something or show something other than who we are. Our parents may have even reinforced this idea within us. Now, we work hard convincing others to believe a projection of ourselves that is not the truth.

Before you reject this idea outright, I'm not saying your mother or father directly told you to lie. In fact, your parents may have done a fine job of living by and teaching you the truth. It is not necessarily in the verbal teaching or lack thereof where you learned not to live by and in truth. In fact, it might not be your parents at all who encouraged you to live or be something other than the truth. It's possible that other people and things you spent more time with than your parents had a major effect on your learning. Your friends, teachers, media, and life experience have likely been more influential. Many, if not all, of these other "teachers" have been working for years to convince you that you have to be someone different from your real self.

That said, moms and dads indeed often teach their kids that they must put on a show. Parents often expect their children to represent something of the parents themselves rather than who and what the children are at their core.

Before you take offense, let me share an example. When your parents were going to have guests over, my guess is they instructed you to clean your room, and the house was to be tidied before the guests arrived. Why? Why did cleaning need to happen right before company was coming? There's nothing wrong with a clean home. But I would argue that parents usually want to portray to their company that this is how their home looks *all the time*. Isn't it an attempt to control embarrassment and falsely appear to be people who customarily have a clean house? The reality for most is that our houses are probably a mess most of the time. Think it over. How many of us have bought into the lie that to be accepted, we cannot share the truth about who we are? Maybe we think if someone saw our messy house, they would feel something negative about us and reject us. Our thinking and acting in ways that are meant to portray something other than the truth is leading to devastating consequences in relationships and destroying hope of genuine intimacy.

When I raised this example with my wife, she challenged it, saying she wasn't sure it held as much weight as I thought it did. She argued that it could be simply that many people like to be hospitable, and part of that is having a clean house. I don't argue that this is true for some. But I wonder, even for these folks, how much of their hospitable behavior is grounded in how they are perceived by others. For example, I've heard it said in my home, "I can't believe someone saw our house like this," after we had a friend over without cleaning the place. I'm quite certain we were as hospitable as can be, and our house wasn't a disaster.

There are many other examples, one of which Tammy supplied. We have a good friend whose parents never welcomed discussion of feelings in the house. In fact, if arguments or any challenges came up in conversation, the parents quickly shut them down. Our friend's family "never had arguments." Trust me, no family exists or has ever existed that hasn't had arguments or disagreements. The very first family on earth had a major argument between brothers that resulted in the death of one of them. Our friend's parents worked hard to present themselves to outsiders and the immediate family as people who didn't argue. This was meant to show that they were different or better than the norm. Further, they were people who kept their feelings to themselves rather than allowing themselves to be known. This is a wrong teaching that many mothers and fathers instill in their children, albeit sometimes unknowingly. Sadly, many learn in this way that they cannot or should not be completely truthful about themselves or their feelings.

The ongoing sagas taking place between people who cannot be truthful are causing profound consequences. I'm not surprised today how many relationships are torn apart and discarded as couples finally realize they have never completely known the actual truth about each other. I feel that the primary reason so many marriages end after roughly a year is because after that time, each partner understands that the person they married is someone different from the person they thought they'd married. The truth has come out. In the courtship phase of their relationships (if we can even call today's premarriage activities courtship), these couples had "fun" and discovered that they enjoyed being together, including sexually; but they did so without doing the hard work of getting to know each other at the core, intimate level.

To compound the problem, men and women often pretend to be something different from who they are at this stage because they are scared to death that if they revealed their true selves, they wouldn't be chosen for the relationship. We need to call this hiding and pretending what it is: dishonesty. It's as if premarriage has become a grand masquerade party, with couples wearing the costumes and face coverings until the marriage ceremony.

In addition, as it relates to truth, I find it interesting how many people don't understand how much they cheat themselves and their sexual partner in the experience of sex. Everyone today, it seems, is focused on achieving "great sex." The focus is on finding the right partner, the right settings, the right activities, and the right methods. Magazine after magazine with helpful ideas about how to have better sex line the checkout aisles of virtually every grocery store. What these individuals don't understand is that they will never experience the grandeur of fantastic sex without really knowing their partner and being known by their partner. And remember, being known is all about truth.

I find it fascinating that the Bible uses the English word *know* to describe men and women having sexual relations. Throughout the Bible, God reminds us, "God is truth." Jesus declared, "I am the way, *the truth*, and the life" (John 14:6, emphasis mine). Why should we find it hard to believe that at the center of life-altering, fantastic sex is truth? Think with me for a moment about the various ways truth can intersect with sex and make a world of difference:

- **Nakedness.** When a husband and wife are naked before each other, there is truth. A person may claim to have an amazing body and may wear clothes that hide their belly fat. But when the clothes come off, no one can hide the extra weight in their midsection. There is an automatic truth built into being naked around someone else; i.e., this is how I really look. It's amazing how much money we spend to hide our nakedness. Now, I'm not suggesting we become nudists, and I'm not at all opposed to lingerie. However, I wonder how often special clothing or other items are requirements for some to have meaningful sex because they are not excited enough by their spouse's nakedness alone.

- **I am desired.** I learned several important things from my counselor when I began my recovery work. I'll never forget this statement, which I wish I had understood before I got married: "If her 'no' doesn't mean 'no,' then her 'yes' doesn't really mean 'yes.'" My counselor helped me realize that my wife has every right to say no to sex whenever she feels the need to do so. If I honor that no and don't push or seek to turn it into a yes, I am showing her that her thoughts, opinions, and sexuality are important to me. Then I will learn just how wonderful her true yes is. What a difference this makes. Rather than simply trying to get me to stop pushing, she is saying, "Yes, I want to be with you. Yes, I love you and desire you." This is especially true in monogamous marital relationships. In such relationships, each partner says whenever they have sex, "I desire you and only you. I have chosen you out of all the other human beings on the planet." This truth makes a world of difference. When yes is true and not simply a decision to pacify our spouse's desires, it really changes things.

- **Sex can be a mess and the relationship can still be as solid as ever.** For those in a relationship not defined by intimacy, this statement may seem ludicrous. But remember, sex doesn't equate to intimacy, so this statement is accurate. If we can all be honest, perfect sex is usually the exception and not the rule in almost every sexual relationship. There are all kinds of things that can go wrong. I wish this was more clearly communicated to those entering into marriage. Stress, poor health, and all kinds of other worldly pressures influence our ability in the bedroom. Additionally, past trauma and present issues can play a role in how "good" sex is. Simple issues such as biologically not being able to perform, being physically exhausted, and the fact that the children will not go to sleep are realities that cause issues in bed. How wonderful it is to know the truth that we are okay, even when things don't go as either of us desires or if sex doesn't happen at all.

- **I am known and accepted.** While this statement
  may be tied or related to nakedness, it is a far
  deeper concept. When my wife is sexual with
  me, she is mentally and emotionally saying, "I
  accept you." Because I am fully known by her,
  this is really an amazing reality. To be frank,
  I'm amazed all the time that I am still wanted,
  at least by my wife. My wife knows the past I
  keep in the deepest recesses of my heart. She
  knows how terrible I can be. She knows things
  that would make others run or shriek in horror,
  and yet she still says, "I accept you." This kind
  of truth makes sex one of the most marvelous
  things life can bring. Without truth, the sexual
  experience is little more than a bodily function
  that triggers endorphins and neurons. These are
  wonderful in and of themselves, but they're so
  much less than what God intended for us.

In polite company, the term I've heard most frequently
regarding sex is either *love,* as in "We made love," or
intimate, as in "We were intimate last night." I can
promise you I have never heard another human being
say, "My wife and I had the most wonderful expression
of truth last night." That statement alone sounds weird,
and I had to reread what I typed. Why is that? Why is it
weird? Such an expression might lead me to believe that
both enormous love and enormous intimacy were likely
involved. In contrast, with the other two expressions,
we actually don't know if either love or intimacy was
part of the physical exercise that took place. The reality
is this: Truth has everything to do with both love and
sex. At least love and sex as God intended.

Intimacy and love are simply not possible apart from rigorous truth. The opposite of truth is a lie. Anything less than truth is, therefore, some variation of a lie. Relationships cannot truly be deep when there are shades of dishonesty present. This seems to go without saying, and I shouldn't even need to expound on it. And yet our actions, I'm afraid, seem to say that I do.

If we are honest, our actions show that we often believe we can hide truth from those we care about, those "marked by very close association, contact, or familiarity" (i.e., "intimate"), according to *Merriam-Webster*.[12] Before you are too quick to write off what I'm asserting here, answer a few questions about yourself:

- What truth about me do my closest friends/ wife/husband not know that, if this truth became known, would totally change the way they look at me?

- Do I have any secrets I will take to my grave and will not share with anyone?

- How many people know my worst character defects?

For me, I realized that, while many people are not safe enough to share information like that with, there are some people who are sufficiently safe to be trusted. Those are the people with whom I want to have relationships that are marked by intimacy.

---

[12]   *Merriam-Webster*, s.v. "intimate," accessed June 14, 2024, https:// www.merriam-webster.com/dictionary/intimate.

And, for that intimacy to occur, I'm going to need to always operate truthfully. This means speaking truth, modeling truth, and resisting the urge to hide from the truth for fear of what will happen. Yes, others might reject me. It's possible that the revelation of my truth might even lead to the loss of the relationship itself. Yet it's also possible that if I am sharing truth in this way, life might become more wonderful than I could have imagined otherwise.

Can you also now see how there can be no intimacy without trust? Truth is a central component of intimacy. However, if you look at the self-evaluation questions I posed above, doesn't each of them have something to do with trust or a lack of it as well?

- There might be truths I don't want my closest friends/wife/husband to know because *I don't trust* the way they would look at me after finding out. They might reject me, not accept me, or, worse yet, hurt me if they knew these truths.

- I can't trust anyone with (whatever secret you are holding on to and won't share with anyone).

- If people knew my worst character defects, there is no way I could trust that they would want to be in a relationship with me. Worse, they might gossip or share these terrible flaws with others, which would lead to my ruin.

In my own case, as I worked my way through counseling and group recovery work, I learned that I had an enormous problem through the better part of my first forty years of life: I did not trust others. Period. This certainly resulted in my unwillingness to be known. In fact, not trusting others made it rare for me to tell the entire truth about a lot of things. By the way, the entire truth is the only truth worth talking about. It took a long time and a lot of work for me to get to the place where I believed I could really be accepted and loved with my truth in the open. Frankly, it took a long time to look at myself in the mirror and speak truthfully about a lot of things, including what I just wrote. When I realized just how much more others trusted me when I was fully truthful, it changed my life. I began trusting others. It changed my relationships. Telling the truth allowed me to have real, intimate relationships with others for the first time in my life. Telling the truth should be easy, right? It's not for some of us.

For many addicts, truth is a real problem. Almost everyone struggles to be 100 percent honest 100 percent of the time. We often believe that minor and insignificant lies don't matter. In fact, some might argue that it's not even possible to always be honest. Among addicts, though, many evolve into great liars. This was true for me. It's difficult to confess, especially as a Christian, but lying has been a struggle for me for most of my life.

My mother and stepfather told my brother and me that we should always be truthful. They told us the outcome of lying would always be worse than that of simply being honest. For me, there were a couple of tremendous problems with this. First, while I heard them saying this, both of them practiced something totally different in real life. My brother and I learned to lie by simply watching them. They lied about all kinds of things, big and small. Second, what they said was not my actual experience most of the time. Because of the abuse I lived with, getting caught in a mistake led to terrible consequences. If I could lie to avoid getting caught or to divert the blame to someone else, the outcome really was *much* better for me. So, I learned early on to stretch the truth or simply lie when it most suited me. This pattern started when I was a boy and, despite my desire to change, simply persisted in my adulthood.

Worse, as I grew into adulthood, lying, it seems, was actually endorsed or promoted. For many years, I've worked in sales-related industries. While it's sad to admit, I've worked with some other superb liars. For example, it's amazing how many salespeople will say something like "I'm going to be in your area next week and would like to stop by and see you." Salespeople use this technique whether or not they actually have appointments scheduled in that area. It's simply a small lie to gain a meeting. You may look at this and think, "That's not that big of a deal." However, it is a matter of character and integrity. It is a matter of whether someone is a person of truth.

Coming out of hiding in the early days of recovery meant a new focus on being honest—always. The little white lies and blame-shifting needed to stop. I changed to operating from a position of 100 percent honesty in every relationship and in every circumstance. This was a lot harder than I thought it would be. Early on, I remember being shocked at how easy it was for me to lie about stuff that didn't matter. When facing guilt about something I had done or hadn't done, my immediate reaction was to deflect this or to lie. Now, I need to be honest and say, "Yep, I blew it." I'm thankful being honest has become easier over the past nine years, although, to this day, I sometimes have to remind myself to tell the truth. Some habits are tough to break.

I've learned that living life in truth is amazingly freeing. I've also learned that many people, especially the ones I care about, will forgive an occasional mistake or error; we all make them. Every single relationship in my life has moved to being more intimate solely because I am always operating from a position of honesty, and because of that, my friends, clients, family, and church trust me. One lie could, and likely would, destroy that.

I've also learned that I'm not alone in my struggles with being honest all the time and that others are often far more understanding than I give them credit for. For example, I'll never forget my interview to serve in deacons' ministry at a church I attended. This occurred several years after I had stepped down from leading a different church as their lead pastor, and it was a test of my ability to live my life in truth. The senior pastor and another elder, who was a good friend of mine, interviewed me the way they did all candidates for service ministry. It's important to understand that both men already knew me well. They knew my story at a pretty deep level.

Toward the end of our meeting, my friend said, "Rob, thanks for allowing yourself to be known. Is there anything else about yourself from a character standpoint that you have not made known?" Wow, what a question! As I paused, the actuality that I had been a habitual liar for most of my life came to mind. We hadn't discussed this during any of our meetings, and while parts of my story had touched on it that day, I had not been perfectly clear about this. My immediate thoughts were: (1) *Should I admit anything?* (2) *The thing I would share will never be known if I don't share it.* (3) *What if I share this part of my story and it causes them to reject me?* And (4) *what I have to share is pretty ugly; what if this forever changes these guys' thoughts about me?* Lest you think I relate in intimacy perfectly, I still struggle and ask myself questions like this when facing hard truths that need to be shared.

Fortunately, I did not let fear win the day. What I shared did change these two men's thoughts about me, though not in the way I expected. They did not reject me. These guys loved and accepted me. These guys appreciated me, knowing I would be bare and honest before them. They naturally asked me more about how I was working on that character defect and encouraged me to keep working on and through it. They also empathized with me. My willingness to be open drew us into more of an intimate relationship. Further, I believe God used my willingness to encourage these gentlemen to be more transparent in their own lives. In fact, my senior pastor later asked me to preach on two different Sundays about the love relationship we can have with each other and God when we allow ourselves to be known. Had I allowed myself to cower in my immediate fears, which told me to do anything but be truthful, who knows how much I and others would have been cheated out of?

Before closing this chapter, I'd like to emphasize one more important fact about truth. In relationships, having truth shared, understood, and accepted deepens the bonds of intimacy, often in ways that could never happen apart from sharing truth. To help you understand this point, I'm sharing one last story that happened within the past year. From the outset, I'm not including this story to brag. But it's good from time to time to share success, especially if it encourages others, as I hope this will do for you. This tale involves both of my primary character defects: pride and dishonesty.

I was selling a small boat, for which I had posted an ad on the internet. Some time had gone by, and I dropped the price by two hundred dollars. Just after that, a man came by to look at the boat. He was thrilled upon inspecting it and was ready to pay me. As he got the cash out of his wallet, he said, "So, you had eight hundred listed, correct?" Well, that was the original price I had posted, but I had just reposted the boat for six hundred dollars. To be clear, two hundred dollars is a big deal to me, and I could have used that extra money. And I *had* originally posted it for eight hundred dollars. And so, it was hard, but I simply had to be truthful. I told him I had just relisted it for less. So he asked me, "What do you want?" We settled on seven hundred dollars, and he thanked me for my honesty.

However, the story doesn't end there. When I went inside, I saw my grown daughter and told her the story. She said, "Dad, I'm so glad you are who you are. You're always the person of integrity. As long as I've known you, you're honest and always do the right thing." Wow! I could feel my chest puff up as my pride said, "Yeah, Rob, you really are great." However, my daughter was mistaken, at least about my past. Maybe she didn't know that for many years her dad wasn't like that. Yet, that didn't make her statement any truer. And because I desire an intimate relationship with my daughter, I felt I needed to tell her the truth. So, I did just that. I told her that for most of my life I was not always truthful. Had this experience happened ten years prior, I might have acted totally differently. I told her that over the past eight years I had been aggressively working on being honest and that even this situation had been tough for me.

You know what happened? My daughter said she was even more proud of me now than she'd been when she'd made the statement. She thanked me for being honest with her, too, and appreciated that I was actively seeking to be a better man. Our relationship went to an even deeper level than it had been before.

Why did I share this story? Because truth, like love, has EVERYTHING to do with intimacy. Love and truth are not secondhand emotions, as the lyrics of Tina Turner's song suggest. They are important foundations in every relationship. We all need to use all of our heart, including the deepest parts of our soul. Yes, our heart can be broken; but a heart that shares truthfully and opens itself to love can also be accepted, nurtured, and made alive. In fact, such honesty and love, fully exposed before another, especially in marriage, can create the special union or oneness we all really want. Truth indeed has everything to do with it.

NEXT STEP

Your next step for this chapter largely depends on how you answered the introspective questions I posed. If you have a very close relationship (married or otherwise) with another person and that person doesn't know an important aspect of your life or past, now is the time to figure out how best to communicate it. If it's something serious or you know it could have serious ramifications for the relationship, please seek a professional Christian counselor for help before taking any action. If you've realized through reading that you're not 100 percent honest 100 percent of the time, your next step is to commit to moving forward to become that way. Become a totally honest person. It really is a choice.

CHAPTER 5

Acceptance and Forgiveness— Willingness and Ability

In the first chapter of the book, I provided my definition of *intimacy*. As we seek to understand acceptance and forgiveness, let's review the definition of *intimacy* to focus on one of its key tenets:

Intimacy is the natural outcome of relationships in which certainty exists between both parties that each person is consistently

- working to know their true self at their core and to be this true self in the presence of the other party, hiding nothing and putting themselves in a vulnerable position;

- aware that they are loved and cared for exactly as they are, inclusive of their own faults, wrinkles, and problems;

- *living, loving, and interacting within an atmosphere of ongoing and mutual forgiveness and acceptance;*

- expressing and openly sharing feelings because the fear of rejection is nonexistent; and

- feeling a regular and consistent closeness that is unique and special—a closeness not shared with anyone else.

Notice I have emphasized "living, loving, and interacting within an atmosphere of ongoing and mutual forgiveness and acceptance" as one of the things we must have certainty of in an intimate relationship. But what does this mean? There are multiple questions we might ask, such as

- Are there limits to this forgiveness and acceptance?

- What does forgiveness look like?

- What does acceptance mean or involve?

- How often must I forgive and accept?

- What if I can't forgive and accept?

- Since the definition includes "mutual," how can I control the other party in the relationship? And what if the other party is unwilling to return forgiveness and acceptance?

These are all significant questions we will examine, at least at the surface level. Any thorough examination of what it means to truly accept and truly forgive another person would require more words than I could supply in one or two chapters. I am not an expert on forgiveness; I simply know what it means to desperately need forgiveness, and what it feels like to receive it. I know how it radically affects relationships because I have seen it affect my relationships. Whenever we experience forgiveness and acceptance in a relationship, it has a tremendously positive effect. Any expertise or wisdom I have related to this topic stems from living life on both sides of the acceptance/forgiveness coin. Today, I am walking in intimacy with others because I have been willing to both forgive and accept myself, *and* because others have forgiven and accepted me. In my life, these two truths have also enabled me personally to forgive and accept others.

It is certainly not my goal in this chapter to thoroughly and completely define what it means to forgive, nor do I have the capacity or wisdom to deal with all the intricacies of the heart that are required to forgive and accept. More simply, my goal is to help you see that intimacy isn't completely possible without both acceptance and forgiveness. In addition, I want to provide a framework for examining our individual willingness to both forgive and accept, as well as our individual ability to forgive and accept. After examining those things, we will consider what it takes in actual relationship settings to actually do so. Equally important, I want to encourage you that mutual forgiveness and acceptance aren't pie-in-the-sky thinking. It is possible to abide in relationships marked by mutual forgiveness and acceptance, and these relationships are radically different from other ones. Mutual forgiveness and acceptance change everything, even in relationships where terrible hurt has taken place between the individuals.

A Willingness to Forgive and Accept

I believe that in order for us to forgive and accept others, we must have a willingness to do so. This appears obvious. We might assume that every human being automatically has such a willingness. But I encourage you to think a little deeper.

Most people have never considered how willing or unwilling they naturally are to accept and forgive others. Any serious consideration of the subject might well begin with facing the existing reasons for not wanting to accept and forgive others. You may find this odd, but the exercise of facing the reasons not to accept and forgive is highly important. It's much like asking an addict to count the cost of giving up their addiction. For us to accept and forgive, we need to examine why we don't in the first place or, at a minimum, why the choice is even that—a choice we must make. Here is a list of reasons you or I might choose *not* to accept and forgive, in no particular order:

- If I accept and forgive, it will open me up to being hurt again.

- Not accepting or forgiving feels like it helps me hold on to various hurts, so I'm protected, in a sense.

- If I accept and forgive, I will no longer have an excuse for feelings I'm holding on to.

- I don't know how to accept and forgive and don't see it as even possible.

- Others have hurt me so badly that they don't deserve to be forgiven.

- Holding on to unforgiveness and things that need to be forgiven makes me feel better about myself.

- It is tremendously painful and exhausting to do the work of forgiveness.

I strongly invite you to take some time and examine the reasons you have for being unwilling to forgive others. As you do, I invite you to consider one additional reason that could be as important as any of those mentioned above. It's possible that, like many people, you've never been specifically taught what forgiveness is and is not. Many of us have never really done extensive work to understand forgiveness. Though it will be only a starting point, I do want to at least provide a context for us to work from.

Over the next few pages, I will discuss not only the need for the willingness to forgive and accept, but the importance of the ability itself to forgive and accept. I'll also be discussing in greater detail what it might take to do so. I bring this up now because I believe there are three fundamental principles about forgiveness that must be understood if we are going to absorb the concept. These principles are interrelated, and what I say about one principle might be equally applicable to and possibly even more true of another. It is necessary to work through each of these three principles to reach a place where we are routinely forgiving and accepting others. Doing so will also help us fully receive acceptance and forgiveness from others.

Principle One: Forgiveness is often not a onetime event.

Especially for the deepest of wounds, forgiveness might not be a onetime event. In fact, most times, forgiveness is an ongoing, moment-by-moment, day-by-day decision— especially for the gravest of sins one person can commit against another. That this fact is true does not mean forgiveness is not possible. It doesn't mean forgiveness has not already taken place. It simply means forgiveness needs to continue to take place.

My wife did not know the real me during the greater portion of our marriage because I kept significant parts of myself completely hidden from her. I did things over that time that significantly hurt her. Ultimately, there came a day when I needed to come clean about who I was and admit to the specific hurts I had done to her. Forgiveness will be a lifelong activity for my wife. After I finally became truthful, she first had to decide whether she would forgive me. She has had to remake that decision many, many times since her original "yes" decision. Sadly, she will probably have to make it many more times in the future. Every time something reminds her of my past sin, she must decide again to forgive me. Just to be clear, I say this not because I am continuing to sin against her in the ways I used to, and I certainly don't believe I will. She needs to continue to forgive simply because the hurt I inflicted on her is never entirely forgettable. For example, a song might come on the radio that reminds her of what I have done against her. It's at those times that she must once again forgive me. Forgiveness truly is a choice.

I really believe both our society and the church are strongly misguided in their understanding of forgiveness. Parents often teach their children to "forgive and forget," as if that is even possible in many situations. Our brains don't work that way. We don't simply forget. We can't make ourselves forget. I, too, have had to forgive myself for the ways I have hurt my wife and others. I've come a long way, but there are still things I hear or see that remind me of my past sin. I have to remember that others have forgiven me, and I have to choose to forgive myself once more.

As we think about our relationships with both ourselves and others, we would be wise early on to think about things from a new perspective: Am I willing to *continue* to forgive? Please don't misunderstand. I don't mean we need to ask, "Am I willing to remain in a position to be victimized, abused, and wounded?" I'm talking about asking ourselves, "Am I willing to deal with how I have been hurt in the past, and choose day by day to continue to forgive?" I'll speak more on this later, but this is a crucial question that needs to be answered honestly.

Principle Two: Forgiveness is often more of a need for us than for others.

This principle may seem backward to you. We often think about forgiveness as if it is almost all about the other person. We've been wronged, so forgiveness helps that person. It frees them. But often, forgiveness is far more about what we are doing in and for ourselves than what we are doing for another person. To be clear, when we forgive someone else, it can and often does seriously and significantly help them. Anyone who has received forgiveness knows how it feels and how freeing it is. When one person has wronged another, there is a break in communion. This communion is required for intimacy. Like it or not, forgiveness is the only way to repair such a break in communion. In an actual sense, forgiveness is the beginning of healing in any broken relationship.

But while forgiveness helps others and helps our relationships with them, it dramatically affects us as well—as much as, if not more than, anyone else involved. My guess is that if we fully understood the extent to which our forgiving others changes us, we would be far more likely to have a willingness to forgive. I believe this was one of a few significant factors that caused me to become willing to be known and get the help I needed to overcome my own addictions.

My understanding of my need for forgiveness became clearest roughly ten years ago when my pastor preached a sermon series on forgiveness. I needed that message, and the Lord used it to begin the changes in me that I also needed. It was through his preaching and through conviction by the Holy Spirit that I knew unequivocally that I needed to be forgiven. At the time of that message, I had little understanding of how greatly forgiveness changes things. I also didn't clearly understand how important it was for me to forgive myself. What I have since learned is that giving forgiveness has profound effects overall on the one who's doing the forgiving. Please consider a few examples of how forgiveness and unforgiveness affect us in extraordinary ways:

- **Unforgiveness keeps us from being forgiven by God.** Jesus's words in the Gospel of Matthew should cause us to think seriously about our choice not to forgive others: "But if you do not forgive others their trespasses, neither will your Father forgive your trespasses" (Matt. 6:15).

- **Forgiveness causes love to abound and friendships to be kept.** I think many who have been forgiven by a friend realize the importance of that forgiveness. I've talked to many people who have received forgiveness, and the result is that their relationship blossomed beyond what they could have ever expected. The Bible puts it like this: "Whoever covers an offense seeks love, but he who repeats a matter separates close friends" (Prov. 17:9). It's far better for us to forgive ("cover") wrongs done against us than to dwell on them by bringing them up over and over again, which will cause separation in the relationship.

- **Our health depends on our ability and willingness to forgive.** Do a quick internet search on the connection between health and forgiveness and you'll find plenty of scientific and medical support for the practice of forgiving yourself and others. For example, did you know that multiple studies have concluded that forgiveness significantly improves both our mental and physical health as we age?[13] Maybe that's why some of the unhealthiest, most frequently sick people I have known were individuals who chose to live lives grounded in anger, resentment, and unforgiveness. Science continues to prove repeatedly that forgiveness is *really* important for our health.

- **Forgiveness allows us to empathize with others.** When we empathize with others, we often gain new perspectives on ourselves. We see our interconnectedness with mankind. It's important to understand that we often are not that different from those who have wronged us. There are dynamic things that happen to us and others when we see ourselves correctly. For example, every time someone cuts me off on the highway and I quickly forgive them because I, too, have cut someone off by mistake in the past, it makes me less angry and far more likely to have an enjoyable rest of my drive.

---

[13]   Justyna Mróz and Kinga Kaleta, "Forgive, Let Go, and Stay Well! The Relationship between Forgiveness and Physical and Mental Health in Women and Men: The Mediating Role of Self-Consciousness," *International Journal of Environmental Research and Public Health* 20, no. 13 (June 26, 2023): 6229. doi: 10.3390/ijerph20136229. PMID: 37444077; PMCID: PMC10341467.

Principle Three: Forgiveness and acceptance are two different things, and you *can* have one without the other.

This last essential principle is critically important. In my mind, it might be one of the most misunderstood aspects of forgiveness, because forgiveness and acceptance are so commonly lumped together. But we must be clear about this: you can forgive and not accept!

As I mentioned earlier, both acceptance and forgiveness are requirements for intimacy. However, there is a very important truth to face up to: intimacy is *not* possible in all relationships, especially as far as forgiveness and acceptance are concerned. Yes, others need forgiveness. Yes, we need for ourselves the ability to forgive others. Yet, that I choose to forgive someone does not automatically mean that I can or should accept them. In fact, I might not, and probably should not, accept certain things someone else has done to me. There are some behaviors and actions that are simply never acceptable.

Any form of abuse is completely unacceptable. A relationship where abuse is present will never be intimate. No person should remain in a relationship where abuse makes its home. Sadly, too many (*one* would be too many, by the way) remain in relationships where abuse occurs because they feel some moral or religious command to do so. We must speak clearly about this and encourage people to get the help they need. Abuse takes many forms, including verbal abuse, emotional abuse, physical abuse, and sexual abuse. Those being abused are victims and often can't think clearly for themselves.

They often can't properly defend themselves. Victims need friends. Usually, they need someone willing to speak the truth in love, the truth that no one deserves harmful treatment of any sort and that help is available. No one should ever "accept" abuse.

Along this line of thinking, I am truly thankful that some people can change. Praise God, I am not the man today that I once was. While someone who has deeply wounded and wronged us might do the work necessary to become a different person, this does not automatically mean that we have to accept them in the future. Sometimes, we, by the grace and help of God, can accept those who have wronged us in terrible ways. I am a living example of what I'm speaking about. My amazing wife chose to both forgive and accept me. It is the clearest presentation of the gospel I have seen, and I am and will remain forever blessed because of it. However, and I wish this were not so, blessed people like me are far more often the exception than the rule.

In many situations, a person can indeed work through forgiveness but, sadly, not get to a place where they can accept being with or being in a relationship with the person who has seriously wronged them. Especially when abuse has occurred, some experiences are simply too traumatic to ever forget or accept, even when the abuser has totally changed. As professionals have conducted more research on trauma, they have found that many terrible emotional/relational experiences can deliver trauma of sufficient magnitude to create post-traumatic stress disorder (PTSD)-type symptoms. In some relationship situations, it is possible, and sometimes better, that the relationship be severed, rather than for a victim or survivor to continue to experience ongoing PTSD stress because of the simple presence of the offender. This is especially true if there is a reasonable likelihood that events will repeat in the future to trigger the victim once more.

While I have received both acceptance and forgiveness from my wife and have lived the wonderful side of the reality I'm talking about, I also write about this from personal experience on the other side. No child wants to sever a relationship with his or her parents. Every boy wants a mom. That's certainly true of me. But the abuse I experienced as both a child and a young man at the hands of my mother was absolutely too much. I could not remain in any kind of meaningful relationship with her. My decision was reaffirmed repeatedly, given that my mother was unwilling or unable to get the help she needed. I could not be assured that the abuse I'd experienced, or some variation of it, wouldn't be repeated. As a husband and father, I have a responsibility to protect my wife and children. The responsible choice was to end our mother-son relationship.

The trauma delivered by my mom was just too real. Even though I ended our relationship, I still have to choose daily to forgive her. It is sad for anyone to say, "I can't be in a relationship with my mom." But making that decision was the only way for me to be healthy. That decision was also vital for me to be in healthy relationships with others. While understanding that we must continue to do the work necessary to forgive others, it is both healthy and fitting for any individual to set appropriate boundaries for themselves. It's also healthy and appropriate to be truthful about what we can and cannot accept.

An Ability to Forgive and Accept

One of the greatest hindrances to a person's having a willingness to accept and forgive is the possibility that the person has never fully experienced forgiveness themselves. As you may infer from what I've talked about thus far, true forgiveness is not very common. We don't habitually forgive; it's not our general go-to. For this reason, many of us are living life without a reference point. That's one reason the gospel message is so profound and so needed. I don't believe anyone who hasn't truly experienced forgiveness and acceptance at a heart level will ever properly be able to accept and forgive others. I know that's a radical statement and you might not accept it. But I really believe it.

The gospel message is radical on a variety of different fronts, any of which by themselves would make us scratch our heads in disbelief. Let's consider a few of them:

- The Bible declares that all of humanity—past, present, and future—has acted and will continue to act in rebellion against a loving God who wants the best for us. The Bible term for this is "sin." Yet, while that is true, God continues to love us and chooses for His own sake to forgive us. He loves us and forgives us while asking nothing of us other than to realize we need His mercy and to accept His forgiveness freely offered through an intimate love relationship with Jesus.

- It is in our very state of living in active sin that God chooses to love and forgive us. Romans 5:8 puts it this way: "But God shows his love for us in that while we were still sinners, Christ died for us."

- Jesus, who is God Himself and the only person who ever lived who didn't rebel against God, willingly sacrificed Himself through the most awful death imaginable so that we can have a restored relationship with God. He did so knowing that the overwhelming majority of people would not want such a relationship. And, in the very process of dying, while those actively involved in His crucifixion were taunting Him, spitting on Him, and further humiliating Him, He uttered this prayer: "Father, forgive them, for they know not what they do" (Luke 23:34).

- No matter how many times we rebel or how egregious the rebellion, God forgives. In fact, God consistently throughout the Bible uses the picture of a bride and groom to represent His relationship with His people. And the picture looks like this: God is the groom, over and over again forgiving and inviting back into fellowship

His bride, who repeatedly is running after anything but her groom who loves her. See most of the Old Testament and multiple references in Hosea for images of this.

• Throughout the Bible, God consistently forgives, and many He chooses are the types of people others reject. He then uses them for His greater purpose. Consider the apostle Paul, who wrote two-thirds of the New Testament epistles. Before his conversion to Christianity, Paul was actively involved in killing Christians because of their faith.

When a human being comes to fully understand the magnitude of the gospel, how wicked at a heart level we all really are, and just how much God loves us, and then receives supernatural forgiveness for all his mistakes, it changes that person. The person is, as the Bible explains, "born again" (John 3:3). In another biblical description of this transformation process, God says, "I will cleanse you. And I will give you a new heart, and a new spirit I will put within you. And I will remove the heart of stone from your flesh and give you a heart of flesh" (Ezek. 36:25–26). Yet far too many people possess a "heart of stone" and are trying to forgive themselves and others from that heart. What they need is a supernatural heart transplant with a new, forgiven heart that is clean and ready to love others well. Part of that loving others well includes forgiving in the same manner that we have been forgiven by God. This, as I see it, is the one thing that makes the greatest difference not only in your willingness to forgive and accept others, but in your ability to do so as well.

NEXT STEP

As with the last chapter, your next step now depends greatly on where you are in your life. Have you ever fully received the love and forgiveness found in a relationship with Christ? If not, that's your next step. Pray and admit to God that you need His forgiveness and want a relationship with Him. Then believe. Receive His forgiveness. Then reach out to a Bible-believing, Bible-teaching pastor of a Christian church to help you more completely understand what living in a forgiven, restored relationship with God looks like. If you don't know where to turn, I invite you to email me directly at **info@RedefiningIntimacy.org**, and I'll help point you forward. If you already know what the Lord's forgiveness feels like, your next step is to deeply consider whether you have forgiven yourself and others, *and* whether you have properly sought the forgiveness of those you have wronged. That's not easy, and depending on what forgiveness is needed, it may require the help of a professional Christian counselor. Commit to getting the help you need to begin walking in forgiveness.

CHAPTER 6

Acceptance and Forgiveness— Accomplishing It

In the last chapter, we examined the reality that in order to forgive and accept others, we must have willingness to do so. But because acceptance and forgiveness rarely come naturally to us, what does it actually take for us to accept and forgive, especially when it seems much easier to hold on to rejection and unforgiveness? I believe that, besides what we have already considered, there are two primary virtues you and I need to develop in order to internalize acceptance and forgiveness: empathy and desire.

In his book *Scary Close*, Donald Miller writes, "The stuff it takes to be intimate is authenticity, vulnerability, and a belief that other people are about as good and bad as we are."[14] We've already discussed the idea of being known and dealing truthfully with ourselves and others. This is what I believe Miller means by "authenticity" and "vulnerability." When I now bring up "empathy," I am connecting with Miller's idea that it takes "a belief that other people are about as good and bad as we are."

If we permit ourselves to be honest, I think many of us sincerely struggle with the notion that others are about as good and bad as we are. For various reasons (mine is pride), we often don't see others as we see ourselves. First, many of us like to think of ourselves as far better than others. "I'm not like that" and "At least I don't do that" become part of our thinking, if not actually part of our vocabulary. There is a large segment of humanity who regularly judge others and view them as worse than themselves. They do this primarily so they feel better about themselves. For years, to deal with the ugliness I felt inside of me, this was the life I led. It was the way I thought. I may not have said as much, but the thoughts and the thought processes were very real. When I finally perceived that others were not all that different from me, I started accepting them more readily. The more I understood that they were not significantly better or worse than me, the more I became willing to accept both them and myself.

---

[14]   Miller, *Scary Close*, 155.

While many of us normally see ourselves as better than others, some of us gravitate toward the other side of this pendulum. We see others as far better than ourselves. In some weird way, for me, this is the reality of what I thought. I know this sounds convoluted, considering that I just said I used to believe I was better than others. For me, the pendulum routinely swung from one side to the other. For example, when I was trapped in my addiction, my shame was overwhelming. I felt alone and that everyone else was better than me. So, to compensate for this and not stay in a constant state of despair, I chose the other side of the pendulum: to think more highly of myself than of others. Because deep down I couldn't accept myself or face the reality that I thought so poorly of myself, I convinced myself the complete opposite was true. And I sought to convince others as well. All of this came from a heart filled with shame. The abuse I suffered as a child traumatized me so thoroughly that I believed I was trash. I was sure I would never really amount to anything. Basically, everyone was better than me—or so I thought.

When I started accepting that others were not all that much better or worse than me, I discovered I could more readily empathize with people. I agree wholeheartedly with psychologists Henry Cloud and John Townsend, who say about empathy, "We literally 'enter the other person's head' and attempt to understand how he feels, what he believes, and how he thinks. Empathy is walking in the moccasins of another person, and not judging him until we can see what suffering he's been through to get to the point he's at."[15]

---

[15]   Henry Cloud and John Townsend, *Safe People* (Grand Rapids, MI: Zondervan, 1995), 44.

This relates directly to acceptance and forgiveness in that, in order to forgive, we need to accept that others have the very same needs that we have. They need forgiveness, just like we need forgiveness. Empathy demands that we connect with not only our feelings but also our failures. In order to forgive, we must accept that we are not much different from anyone else. Others make the same dumb, careless mistakes we make. Yes, we can sometimes be self-centered, but so can others. All of us are far guiltier than we readily want to admit. We all need forgiveness.

When we choose to stop and connect with those feelings and be mindful of our own failings, it enables us to connect with others who need and deserve forgiveness. We become more willing to accept others after these moments. Because we realize we, too, want and need to be accepted, our empathy fuels our acceptance of others.

Anyone who's honest about this subject will readily admit that this is often terribly difficult. We don't want to face ourselves. None of us want to connect with those feelings. We don't want to do the hard work that acceptance and forgiveness demand. It's often uncomfortable and quite painful connecting with such things in ourselves. Further, some of us have such deep wounding that even to properly empathize with others will require a lot of help. (Again, I would like to bring up the great work that trained counselors, psychologists, and social workers do. For many people, becoming able to forgive and accept begins with getting professional help to deal with past hurts and feelings that have never been dealt with.)

I discussed in the last chapter how we must have a willingness to forgive, so you might think I have already covered "desire." However, I propose that there can be, and often is, a significant difference between willingness and desire. See, I might be willing to eat a barbecued pork steak, which Tammy loves but I don't really care for. But I promise you, I don't desire pork steaks. I'd much rather have a brat, a hamburger, or, even better, a real steak! But can I move from simply being willing to eat the pork steaks with my wife to desiring to do so with her because I know it will make her happy? When I talk about desiring to forgive and accept, I am really encouraging us to understand that we need to move from a simple willingness toward having a regular desire to forgive and accept. There is a difference.

At the outset, this whole concept probably doesn't seem to make sense. You might think, *If I desire to forgive and accept, doesn't that mean I'm also desiring to be hurt or wronged so I can then forgive? Why would I ever desire that?* These are legitimate questions.

If that's where your mind went, I get it. But part of acceptance is coming to terms with reality—not necessarily wanting that reality. For example, the reality of life is that I'm going to have great days and I'm also going to have really crappy days. I'd like to hope the drive to my office every day will be peaceful and no one will cut me off, fly by me, drive like a maniac, or otherwise demonstrate that their driver's license should be revoked. But there are drivers on the road who ordinarily drive like idiots, just as there are other drivers like me, who also make mistakes when we drive. Part of my acceptance is saying to myself, "This is going to happen."

Where desire meets that acceptance is not that I desire those drivers to drive like that, but my desire needs to be related to what I can control. I can control my responses and my actions. I need to have a desire that says that when those things occur, my choice is going to be to forgive. I need to get to a place where I not only have a willingness, but I have a "want" to be forgiving because I know it's better for everyone— including me. I will speak for myself. I'm inherently selfish. A desire to both forgive and accept needs to come first from within. Desire will grow in me as I see forgiveness and acceptance not as something I should do, but as something I want to do because of how good it is for me.

Desire is more related to our recognition of what is ultimately best and making a conscious choice to live as a person who routinely accepts and forgives others. It's a funny thing; the more we live that way, the more our disposition becomes attuned to being that way. Living this way becomes a habit. It's a way of life. This way of life is refreshing for us, and for others. It's so needed by more of us in the world today.

My grandmother, Rose Gion, passed away at the ripe age of ninety-nine. There were a couple of hundred people at the celebration of life held in her honor, and most were not family members. Over and over, we heard from individuals who spoke about the selfless love my grandma shared. One quality commented on by a great number of people was how forgiving she was. It was her life. She had a desire to forgive others because she saw this as a springboard to sharing the gospel. She loved talking about how much she had been forgiven. This really was her desire. And it radically changed thousands of lives. I say thousands because each of the lives she touched then proceeded to touch other lives. There is no way of telling how many people she influenced over a life of ninety-nine years.

So, why don't we desire to be accepting and forgiving? Again, there are lots of reasons. Some of them relate to the same reasons we are unwilling to be that way. I'd like to point out three reasons I believe really influence whether we will desire to forgive and accept. These are good for us to think about from time to time and may require us to act on them.

1. **Consistent, ongoing hurt erodes our desire to be accepting and forgiving.** If we are in a relationship where another human being knows his actions are hurting us and he keeps performing those actions, it naturally causes us not to want to accept this person's apology. It often leads to a desire to do just the opposite. Rather than having a desire to accept and forgive, we want to reject and hold resentment. But remember, if you are being

consistently hurt by another person and that
person is not making genuine efforts to change,
including making real amends for the hurt
they have caused, you still need to forgive for
your own sake.

2. **If we base our actions on the actions or
    responses of others, we will probably lose
    our desire to accept and forgive.** There is a
    recovery principle I learned a long time ago:
    Control what you can control. You and I may
    not like it, but we cannot control anyone else.
    We certainly can't control whether someone
    truly seeks our forgiveness. And we can't
    control whether another party will forgive us
    after we have apologized and sought his or her
    forgiveness. If you and I are honest, though,
    sometimes we feel like "Why should I forgive
    him when he won't forgive me?" Worse yet,
    we may sometimes think our accepting and
    forgiving others is not recognized. Even worse
    than that, our forgiveness may encourage
    unacceptable behavior in others. If we are
    going to forgive or not based on anything
    another person will or won't do, we are likely
    not to have a desire to be an accepting and
    forgiving person. As I've said before, we must
    desire to be accepting and forgiving for what
    it does for us, even if others don't receive or
    respect it.

3. **If we have never seen acceptance and forgiveness modeled, the process will seem foreign, and we gravitate toward things we know.** We desire things we have experienced and liked. I would not desire a delicious steak if I hadn't experienced the blessing of having a fantastic piece of meat prepared expertly. Growing up, many of us did not live in homes where forgiveness and acceptance were modeled. In fact, it might have been just the opposite. For people who haven't seen acceptance and forgiveness well modeled, desire might need to start by envisioning what we believe this would feel like for ourselves and then seeking to bless others that way.

At the end of the last chapter, I spoke of the forgiveness and acceptance we receive from God. It is through our intimate relationship with God that the desire I've been talking about comes. The more we realize how much we've been forgiven and how good it is to be accepted, the more natural it becomes for us. We will long to be that way with others as we long to be more and more like Christ. And, as a benefit, the Holy Spirit provides guidance in how to do just that. This whole process is life-changing, both for us and for others.

I'd like to simply remind you as I close this chapter that all aspects of forgiveness and acceptance are possible. I speak from experience. I never would have believed I would get to a place where I could fully empathize with people and desire to accept and forgive them.

It seemed impossible. Let me assure you it's not. If I can do it, you can do it. Acceptance and forgiveness are essential to intimacy, and you can find intimacy with others.

NEXT STEP

Your next step for this chapter is to consider those you ordinarily share life with—your coworkers, friends, neighbors, classmates, and so on. Honestly ask yourself whether you feel that any are significantly better or worse than you. Commit right now to seeing others as similar to you—no better and no worse. As you communicate with these folks in the coming weeks, see what happens in your relationships. See if you are able to empathize with the various things they are going through, and see what that does for both of you.

CHAPTER 7

What Can I Control?

When I think about how I thought and lived for the majority of my adult life, it's no wonder I was not experiencing intimacy with others. Sadly, most of my life operated exactly the opposite of most of the things I'm sharing with you in this book. As my life continually spiraled out of control, I tragically remained fixated on trying to control other things and other people. Control and manipulation were my go-to tactics for survival.

Growing up, I learned from my mother and stepfather to control and manipulate others. Whether it was directly through their manipulation and control of me as a boy, or in how my parents lied, hid, fabricated, and performed for others, I learned that things and people could be controlled. If I could not control others, I could at least strongly manipulate them to my benefit. Frankly, I knew of no other way to live. I could not imagine anything else.

Living life this way was exhausting. Worse, there was an inverse reaction that always seemed to play out. The more I sought to control things and others, the less control I had over myself and my own circumstances. It's really weird how that works. I always thought I was a master at control. I wasn't. Far from it. My life reflected anything but control. And while I thought I was controlling others and outcomes, I got lucky at best when things worked out the way I hoped or intended.

Before discussing the integral part that control plays in intimacy, I'd like to dig a little deeper into a variety of ways that we as humans seek to control situations and others. I strongly feel that all of us are far more guilty in this area than we would like to believe. As I share, I invite you to examine yourself and how you may have a habit of seeking to control or manipulate others. (To be clear, the two words are basically synonymous.) Don't be too quick to say, "That's not me." Rather, it's far better for you and me to consider, "How is this me?" Consider the following elements that might be tempting to control.

Others' Feelings

Almost all of us seek, at a minimum, to influence each other's feelings. While there are times when such influence may not be terrible (for example, when we're trying to cheer someone up), manipulation and control certainly are. We can manipulate or control other people's feelings by simply communicating what we believe a person should feel. We can also hide truth or facets of truth to make people feel differently than they would if they knew the whole truth. Feelings can also be controlled by improperly making another person feel bad about how his feelings might influence you or someone else. We often do not realize the many subtle ways people manipulate others' feelings. Often, the manipulation is done with the express purpose of making things better for the controlling party. In these instances, we seek to control and manipulate others without realizing it.

Others' Emotions

Emotions are closely tied to feelings, but they certainly can be different. Emotions are our normal bodily reactions to experiences we encounter. Feelings typically take those emotions and apply to them our thoughts or perspectives on both the emotions and the experiences that led to the emotions. We may attempt to control or manipulate both feelings and emotions so that the outcome is better for us.

For example, American society teaches many boys that the active emotion of crying is a sign of weakness. Crying is an expression of a natural emotion. It should trouble us that any person is discouraged from expressing a God-given emotion. Tying an emotion to something considered bad or of lesser value is a way of manipulating or controlling that emotion. Most of us have been manipulated to either share or not share our emotions. As with controlling others' feelings, there are also subtle ways we might seek to control another person's emotions without even thinking twice about it. For example, for years, I almost never wanted to see a sad or heart-wrenching movie with my wife. Why? I didn't want her to experience and express the emotions that would naturally follow. This may have been driven by caring for Tammy and wanting her to stay happy. But, more likely, I probably thought her emotions at the bad ending of the movie would affect her desire to be pleasing to me. In either case, my goal, in a twisted way, was to try to control her emotions.

Others' Actions

It is tempting, and very easy, to attempt to assert control when you think you know better or are convinced you are the expert. Looking back over the relationship I have with my son, I remember a time when I wanted to control his actions even though he was old enough to make his own decisions. My intentions were good; I knew that at a later time in life he would likely come to regret the decisions he was making. But they were *his* decisions to make—not mine. I put pressure on him and sought to manipulate things for him to see it my way. For example, when he wanted to quit wrestling, I pointed out many reasons why he shouldn't: he would be hurting his team, the school, and me as a coach. My goal at the time was simply to control his actions and his decision, and it hurt our relationship. It would be wise for us always to remember that every human being has his or her own free will. No matter how much we might want to, we can never fully control another person's actions.

Others' Forgiveness

As I noted earlier, we can't control another person's forgiveness or acceptance of us. Yet we often do try to control or manipulate this. With that said, I want to share that there is a big difference between control and influence when it comes to forgiveness. While we can't ultimately control whether someone chooses to forgive us, we can, with our actions, positively and fairly influence their decision to do so or not. There is nothing wrong with that. We can be genuine, seek to make amends, change, empathize, and learn from our mistakes. These are effective ways to influence someone to move to a place of forgiveness and acceptance. However, we can't make someone forgive us, and we must accept that. Whether someone chooses to forgive us is entirely their choice.

Others' Desires

Especially in the closest of relationships, we want others to be aligned with our own thinking and, specifically, our own desires. That way, we are seeking to achieve our goals together. There's nothing inherently wrong with this. But it's not realistic to think our desires will always align. Often, because we are unique individuals, we have very different desires. In the most intimate of relationships, that fact changes nothing. In fact, we can learn to appreciate the differences in our desires.

For years in my marriage, I wronged my wife by frequently seeking to manipulate her desires. In fact, I am aware of myself enough today to know that trying to control my wife's desires can still be a problem for me. All too often, I approached decisions *I* had made or things *I* thought were best as what was right for *us*. So, that meant I simply needed to get Tammy to desire what I wanted. Some might say, "Rob, you were only trying to influence her." But in truth, I was working to manipulate her to my way of thinking. I could apply pressure I knew would make her feel bad about not being agreeable. Can I share something? In almost every situation when I did that, and we were not in unified agreement without my seeking to control her desires, it worked out terribly. Oh, how I wish I had understood years ago that I had no business trying to control anyone else's desires. Many people camouflage control and manipulation under the word *influence*. For the sake of intimacy, we need to stop.

Others' Beliefs

We should always remember that everyone is entitled to their own beliefs. This other person may be wrong, right, misinformed, or on target in your opinion, but their beliefs are their beliefs. Where we often make the mistake is in assuming we are always right. Whether or not we admit it, we take issue when someone else believes something opposite of what we believe. Some of us cause far more harm than good by trying to force, control, or manipulate others to believe our beliefs the exact way we believe them. Why is it that so many young people leave home and then outright reject so many of the things taught by their parents? I'm sure there are many reasons, but I'll share one: many parents try to control what their kids believe rather than teach them and show them why the parents' beliefs are right. What I am communicating is that we can't control *any* other person's beliefs—even those of our own kids. We can only influence another person's beliefs, and this is especially true of our children. Parents are in an ideal position to do so and must take seriously the role that God has given them.

By the way, I've found that a funny thing happens when I don't try to control others' beliefs, but simply teach and show why I believe what I do. Often, others gravitate toward what I believe. I've seen this in my kids. Tammy and I have done a pretty good job as parents in this area. Our kids clearly know what we believe and why. But we didn't push them or try to control them in their beliefs. What's happened over time is that more and more we find that they are holding beliefs very similar to ours. Amazing how that happens.

Now that we've taken a look at the things we cannot or should not control, let's review why. There are two primary reasons why controlling another person is destructive to intimacy:

1. **Controlling another person means you do not accept them as they are.** It means you do not trust them. We've already addressed how important trust and acceptance are to intimacy. When we accept another human being and don't seek to control them, we communicate that they have dignity for who they are. We communicate that we trust them. This is the same whether we are talking about their feelings, beliefs, emotions, or forgiveness. If we truly accept and trust another person, they can believe whatever they want to believe, and we don't see it as a threat. They can share whatever emotion is real to them and feel whatever feeling is natural. If, however, we feel that we need to control their beliefs, feelings, and emotions, we really are communicating that we don't accept them and we don't trust them. When this happens, control and manipulation enter the picture and always work actively against intimacy.

2. **No one likes to be controlled.** This almost goes without saying. We hate being controlled by anyone. In my opinion, this is a primary reason why most will not enter into a personal relationship with God. Because people rightly know that a requirement in a relationship with God will be to give control of their lives to Him, they are content living outside that relationship. Humans resist control. We want freedom.

We want to do whatever we want. So, when another human being even attempts to control us, we fight it. We build walls to prevent that control from happening. When we do these things, we create natural barriers to intimacy. Intimacy requires connection with another person, not walls between you and that person. It is impossible to be in an intimate relationship with someone who wants to control you.

With that communicated, there is one last important reality connected to the concept of control that calls for serious attention. While we must not control others in relationships, we must control ourselves.

I have admitted to chronically trying to control and manipulate others. All the while, I had very little control over myself. I can't imagine how much better a person I would be had I spent half the energy and effort I did on controlling others on controlling myself instead. I certainly would have been a much better husband, father, and friend. The amount of debt I've accrued would be radically different had I simply controlled how I spent money. I can look at area after area of my current life and see how it would be better if I'd tried to control myself sooner.

By not doing so, I brought problems and difficulties on both myself and others, which prevented intimacy from happening. How? At a minimum, I communicated to others that I could not be trusted. Whenever we fail to control ourselves, we show others we can't be trusted.

Over the past eight years, I've routinely volunteered in addiction recovery ministry, primarily working with men who identify themselves as sex addicts. Some of these men may not believe they are addicts, but they will at a minimum confess that they struggle with living holy lives in their sexuality. With married men, I've frequently and consistently shared this truth: you must control yourself, or there is no way you will have an intimate love relationship with your wife. The saying "control what you can control" certainly applies here. A wife who can't trust her husband will not be in an intimate relationship with him. She may stay in the marriage for various reasons, including concern for her own well-being and/or to protect her children, who might be hurt if the relationship were severed. But the relationship and the marriage will not be intimate. Men can control whether they look at porn or lust after other women. It may take help, healing, and learning new ways of living life, but it is possible.

I believe it has become far too easy to blame a lot of our problems on a perceived "fact" that things are outside our control. Some blame their weight problems on the fact that they can't control their food intake. Some blame their debt on the fact that they can't control their need to spend money. Many men blame their lust and their use of pornography on God. After all, they surmise, they can't control that God made males primarily visual beings. For me, after really trying on my own for years to stop using porn, I wrongly believed porn was my "thorn in the side" that would always be there, so I'd always fail. These so-called facts are nothing but lies. We really can control more of ourselves than we think we can. Granted, it takes time, work, the help of others, and developing new habits. But we can control whether we take in only what our bodies need rather than go back for multiple helpings. We can control whether we stick to a strict budget. How we think sexually about others and where we put our desire and focus is completely within our control. Quite simply, we can control, and need to control, more of ourselves.

Related to this discussion of control and trust, I want to point out that it doesn't take much to ruin trust. When there has been a breach of trust, it usually takes a long time to repair the damage, assuming trust is reparable at all. Unfortunately, I don't think many of us truly believe this. At least, our actions don't show that we do. I think, especially in the church, we often believe that because a person is called to forgive us, the consequences of the harm we have done won't naturally follow. On the contrary, for EVERY breach of trust, there are real consequences. And for significant breaches, the consequences are that much more extreme.

This line of reasoning applies to all trust breach issues—not just those of a sexual nature. If we lie, we show we can't be trusted. We betray the trust of the person we lied to. If we manipulate, we show we can't be trusted and undermine the trust of the person we manipulated. When we cannot accept and forgive, we breach trust. In every situation where trust has been broken, at least one consequence is that our relationship will not be—and might never be—as intimate as it could have been.

A Final Warning and Encouragement to Control What You Can Control

In my early days of volunteering in recovery ministry, I met a man who ultimately became a good friend. He became quite upset about something that was happening to a fellow group member I'll call Ron. Ron was a great guy who, for years, had been lying to his wife about his persistent use of pornography. His wife had forgiven him and accepted him back into a sexual relationship several times based on his commitment to getting help. She rightfully expected that he would permanently stop using pornography. But after being good for a period of time, Ron always went right back to his old ways, including lying about his behavior. All of this happened before my friend and I ever came to know Ron.

Many people who suffer from addiction make multiple promises they don't keep. That was the case for me. It was also the case for Ron. There was not a heart change in Ron's life, and before long he was using again. Once more, his wife caught him involved with pornography and lying about it. This time, she told Ron to leave and informed him that she would not accept him back in the home. It was at this point that Ron believed he'd hit bottom and finally got serious about changing his life. He learned he was using sex as his drug to cope with life's problems. My friend and I saw a dramatic change in Ron from that time on. He became a new man. He was sorrowful and sought to make amends for the wrongs he had committed against his wife and children.

Ron's wife said she had forgiven him. Even so, she could not allow him back into their marriage relationship or back into the home. Their marriage was shattered. Ron had also lost the trust and respect of his grown children. It wasn't long after that when other consequences occurred. Ron's marriage officially ended in divorce. His house was sold. Ultimately, he had to move out of state to find work and a fresh start. He now needed to restart life.

My friend couldn't understand what was going on and how Ron's wife could not accept Ron one more time. "Surely," my friend said, "she should be able to see how different Ron is now." Ron truly was implementing healthy practices to stay away from his drug. He was living as a changed man. My friend questioned whether Ron's wife truly had forgiven him.

I told my friend what I shared in chapters five and six—that forgiveness and acceptance are two different things. There are consequences of serious breaches of trust. Some wounds and hurts are so deep and so painful that, while they may be forgivable, the trauma and pain may never go away. That trauma and pain might require separation and protection so future healing can occur. That's one important reason it is so necessary that we control ourselves and take our sin seriously.

I don't know what Ron's wife experienced during this situation, and I sure don't know what she experienced in the years prior. I don't know if she ever forgave Ron or not. What I do know is that the ultimate consequence of Ron's inability to control himself was the loss of his marriage and an immediate loss of the trust and respect of his children.

Please understand, I rightfully believe God hates divorce. However, I think it is understandable that there can be such significant wounding—especially in cases of abuse, neglect, or marital unfaithfulness—that divorce becomes necessary for healing to take place. I believe that's why Jesus Christ gave this as a reason for divorce in Matthew 5:32. It is time men and women took seriously the grievous impact of sin, especially serious breaches in trust, like marital infidelity.

That being said, my story could have been the same as Ron's. Nine years ago, my wife had every right to divorce me. I had hurt her and betrayed her numerous times. Actually, because of my years of hiding, I was, at my core, someone she hardly knew. I'm certain the only reason we stayed together is because of God's grace, the amazing love and grace Tammy showed me, and my commitment to consistently pursuing intimacy in our relationship.

I think it's also important to recognize that when I finally got help, I was the one who started being honest and truly desired to get well. Of course, that credit ultimately goes to God, but God provides us with opportunities to choose what we will do. You can control what you will do with opportunities presented to you. You can begin the process of honestly confessing to others where and how you've wronged them. Those first steps may lead to your developing intimacy in your most important relationships, rather than losing everything.

Controlling the things I could control became an important truth for me to live by. It was essential that I believe that with help I could be successful in doing that. Initially, I don't know if I fully believed I could control myself in the long term. I was encouraged to ask myself whether I could control myself for the next ten seconds. Then, ten seconds later, ask myself the same question. Ultimately, a bunch of ten-second increments have added up to nine years. Practicing habits of holiness, seeing others as beautiful individuals created in the image of God, living in honesty, seeking to control myself, and limiting my attempts to control anything other than myself have led to a solid belief and understanding that I can control myself today. Thankfully, I have been able to control myself in my sexuality despite at least thirty years of not doing so before. The result, along with sharing an intimate relationship with my wife, has been amazing and life-transforming. This is possible for you as well. All things are possible with and through the love of God in Christ Jesus, our Lord.

NEXT STEP

Your next step for this chapter is to examine yourself. Ask yourself the following questions and determine whether changes are needed. Are you right now attempting to control others in any way? Are you controlling yourself as you should? What practical steps could you take to release your desire to control others and get a firmer grip on controlling yourself? Will you start taking those steps?

CHAPTER 8

The Need to Feel

Have you ever heard of the disease "congenital insensitivity to pain with anhidrosis" (CIPA)? I hadn't before my work preparing to speak at seminars on intimacy. CIPA is a disease that makes children unable to feel or to sweat. This terrible disease results in more than half of the children with CIPA dying before the age of three from overheating alone. Long before anyone knew about this disease, there was an understanding that being able to feel was vitally important to our health. In truth, we need to feel to survive.

Doctors and nurses know connecting a newborn to her mother as soon as possible after birth makes an enormous difference in the health and wellness of both the mother and the baby. In fact, many studies have shown that infants who experience human touch shortly after birth begin life in a much stronger position than their peers who don't have this advantage. Studies proving this first began in the 1950s, when in 1958 John Bowlby shared the results of his study on "The Nature of the Child's Tie to His Mother" in the *International Journal of Psycho-Analysis*.[16] Multiple other studies on this topic have been conducted since, and all have come to the same conclusion: babies desperately need loving, nurturing human touch.

More recently, many additional studies have affirmed significant benefits for both mom and dad from early and repeated touch between them and their baby. Mood, behavior, and sleep all improve for the baby's parents. For example, Kerstin Uvnäs-Moberg, Linda Handlin, and Maria Petersson show that the release of the hormone oxytocin naturally occurs from this touch and has many positive effects for both baby and parents.[17] Thus, there is certainly good reason to get newborn babies in the arms of their mothers as soon

---

[16]   John Bowlby, "The Nature of the Child's Tie to His Mother," *International Journal of Psycho-Analysis* 39, no. 5 (September/October 1958): 350–73. PMID: 13610508.

[17]   Kerstin Uvnäs-Moberg, Linda Handlin, and Maria Petersson, "Self-Soothing Behaviors with Particular Reference to Oxytocin Release Induced by Non-noxious Sensory Stimulation," *Frontiers in Psychology* 5 (January 12, 2015): 1529. doi: 10.3389/fpsyg.2014.01529.

as possible in the delivery room. Infants and their mothers both need to feel each other.

Even as we grow, our ability to feel remains vital to our health and happiness. It's our ability to feel that keeps us from severely burning ourselves when our skin gets close to hot objects. It's our ability to feel that tells us to put on a coat so we don't freeze. Our ability to feel allows for needed refreshing, like wading in a cool stream on a hot summer day. Feeling allows us to receive joy when we experience the unique texture of a beautiful flower and comforts us when we pull a silk shirt over our skin.

Not only is our ability to feel through the use of the receptors in our skin vital to our physical health, but feeling is also very important in our day-to-day physical relationships. Unless someone has been so severely physically abused that the loving touch of another human triggers past trauma, almost every person benefits from the touch of others. For those in a marriage relationship, the loving touch of their spouse is crucial to their marital intimacy. Obviously, sex can, and should, be part of this touch experience for married couples, but it's not the only touch necessary. In fact, it's probably not the primary touch required. My wife needs to feel me holding her hand. Most wives need to feel the loving caress and arms of their husbands holding them, which uniquely say, "I love you."

There is something special and uniting that happens when a person receives a hug, especially in times of pain or hurt. Fortunately, giving and receiving hugs is not something only married people can do. Every human being has the same opportunity to receive the blessing of a hug and to give this blessing to others. There is nothing like the loving hug of a good friend. It really can change everything, including the intimacy in that simple friendship. When you have time, do a quick online search on "benefits of hugs" or "benefits of hugging." You'll be amazed at how many excellent articles are out there that provide scientific evidence for the many significant benefits for those who hug.

For example, here are just a few of the positive results we experience, according to several studies:

- Holding and hugging reduces stress.[18]

- Hugging makes us healthier, helping prevent illness and infection.[19]

- Hugging can decrease pain.[20]

- Hugging can ease depression.[21]

- Hugging and brief touching may help reduce fear and anxiety.[22]

---

[18]   Tristen Inagaki and Naomi Eisenberger, "Neural Correlates of Giving Support to a Loved One," *Psychosomatic Medicine* 74, no. 1 (January 2012): 3–7. doi: 10.1097/PSY.0b013e3182359335. Epub 2011 Nov 9. PMID: 22071630.

[19]   Sheldon Cohen et al., "Does Hugging Provide Stress-Buffering Social Support? A Study of Susceptibility to Upper Respiratory Infection and Illness," *Psychological Science* 26, no. 2 (2015): 135–47. https://doi.org/10.1177/0956797614559284.

[20]   Julian Packheiser et al., "A Systematic Review and Multivariate Meta-analysis of the Physical and Mental Health Benefits of Touch Interventions," *Nature Human Behaviour* 8 (April 8, 2024): 1088–1107, https://doi.org/10.1038/s41562-024-01841-8.

[21]   Packheiser et al., "Touch Interventions."

[22]   Sander Koole, Mandy Tjew A Sin, and Iris Schneider, "Embodied Terror Management: Interpersonal Touch Alleviates Existential Concerns among Individuals with Low Self-Esteem," *Psychological Science* 25, no. 1 (2014): 30–37, https://doi.org/10.1177/0956797613483478.

Don't you feel you want those benefits? Are they needed in your relationships? I think we all know the correct answer is "Absolutely!" Guess what? Those benefits only happen because of our ability to physically feel the touch of another person. They cannot happen without it.

There are three other considerations related to feeling touch through something as simple as a hug that are worth considering. First, the loving touch of another human being costs nothing. There isn't a price to pay. I can give my best friend a hug the next time I see him, and it would almost certainly benefit him more than if I bought him a hundred-dollar meal. Second, touching or hugging is easy. In fact, most of the time, it's quite natural. It doesn't take much work other than making the commitment to express that I care for another human being. Finally, it not only benefits the receiver, it benefits the giver as well. How often is it that you hug someone and don't get a hug back? Almost never, right? What an amazing thing God has given us to share with each other.

For as long as I can remember, I've been a hugger. I love giving and receiving hugs. I think the primary reason for this is that I was so deprived of healthy, loving touch growing up. I think my body learned to recognize and crave the benefits of a hug without my consciously knowing what was happening. As I understand intimacy more, it has only increased my longing to hug and touch the people I care about.

When I think about the past several years, I've realized that in certain ways I've been down. Yes, I've experienced significant negativity in various aspects of business and even church life. I've lost precious loved ones. But something else with major impact occurred—COVID-19. You may not have thought about this aspect of it, and I hadn't until editing this chapter, but one of the significant things that happened to all of us as we navigated the pandemic is that we, as people, have grown apart physically. Now, we are far more careful about who and how we touch. I remember in the early days of COVID practicing the "side hug." Experts said that to prevent the spread of the virus, we should engage side-by-side, putting our arm around someone's shoulder, rather than giving a traditional frontal hug. I wonder how much of the negativity and depression experienced worldwide during and after the pandemic has stemmed from our craving for physical touch.

While all this is valid, if I wrote a chapter on the need to feel and spoke only of physical touch, I would be doing a great disservice to you. While it is a wonderful gift to feel through our sense of physical touch, God has blessed us with so many other ways we need to feel. Physical touch is crucial and vitally important to us, but there are more ways to feel that are equally life-giving and important to our health and well-being. They relate to the use of the heart more than the skin. I'm talking about using our hearts and heads by sensing through our feelings and emotions.

As I wrote that just now, I wondered if my male readers would immediately close the book. I'm thinking of the scene in the movie *The Princess Bride* where the sick-in-bed grandson tells his grandpa to quit reading the story when Grandpa gets to the part about the characters Westley and Buttercup falling in love and sharing a kiss. For a good proportion of the male sex, the use of our feelings doesn't seem normal. Feeling, men think, is something only women should do. After all, men don't feel. We fight and hunt. We've even coined the term *chick flicks* for the types of movies that pull the heartstrings.

But is it true that men are really not meant to feel? No! I realized one thing quickly in my early days in group recovery work. Men genuinely struggle with communicating their feelings. I did and still do, even though I've been working on it for the past nine years. Ask most men how they're doing or how they're feeling and 90-plus percent of the time you're going to hear "Okay." But it's not only guys that struggle. We *all* struggle with both allowing ourselves to feel and expressing those feelings. Did you know that according to the "Emotions List & Emotional Literacy" resource on the Six Seconds website, a nonprofit organization whose mission is to increase the world's emotional intelligence, "There are some 3000 words for feelings"?[23] How many are you familiar with?

Before I get into why expressing our feelings and emotions along with properly receiving others' feelings and emotions is absolutely critical to

---

[23]   "Emotions List & Emotional Literacy," Six Seconds, accessed June 14, 2024, https://www.6seconds.org/emotional-intelligence/topics/emotions-list/.

intimacy, I'd like us to consider Jesus for a moment. I know Jesus is probably nowhere close to the person you immediately think of when thinking about expressing feelings. But is that fair?

I've been fortunate to watch the television series *The Chosen*. It recreates the Gospel accounts of Jesus and imagines what it might have been like to be in Jesus's presence. Characters in *The Chosen* dress and talk like they probably would have two thousand years ago during the earthly ministry of Jesus. The script writers replaced the "thees and thous" of the King James Version of the Bible with how Jesus and his followers likely talked. One thing I appreciate the most about the show is that in it, Jesus is human. He laughs, cries, and jokes with those He interacts with. You see His emotions and feelings. I think this is one reason why those who otherwise would not pick up a Bible will watch this show.

I bring this up only because, at least in the sense of accurately portraying Jesus, the show really is good. Christians understand and believe that Jesus was Himself both fully God and fully man. On earth, in human form, Jesus was fully a man. He lived, breathed, hurt, and, yes, felt like we all do. As Christians, we are called to be Christlike; literally, imitators of Christ.

I really like how best-selling author Philip Yancey describes both the vulnerability of Christ and His willingness to share His emotions and feelings. In addition to briefly examining some of the range of Jesus's emotional responses, Yancey recalls, "I once attended a men's movement retreat designed to help men 'get in touch with their emotions' and break out of restrictive stereotypes of masculinity. As I sat in a small group, listening to other men tell of their struggles to express themselves and to experience true intimacy, I realized that Jesus lived out an ideal for masculine fulfillment that nineteen centuries later still eludes most men. Three times, at least, he cried in front of his disciples. He did not hide his fears or hesitate to ask for help. . . . How many strong leaders today would make themselves so vulnerable?"[24]

I wholeheartedly agree. That's one reason why, when I facilitate seminars in churches on intimacy, I usually make the following statement: "One way you can be most like Jesus is by regularly sharing your feelings." That should not sound surprising to you. Scripture is rife with example after example of Jesus's feeling, and then acting on or sharing those feelings. How would His disciples, who wrote about their experiences, know what Jesus was feeling unless He shared it? Here's a small sample to illustrate my point.

Jesus Shared Compassion

Jesus frequently showed compassion. In my study of God's Word, I learned that the Greek word often translated as "compassion" means a feeling of "sensation in the guts." It's a deep feeling of pity that literally pains our stomach. It comes from a place of empathy, care, and desire for things to differ from the way they are. Jesus allowed Himself to feel like that.

---

[24]   Philip Yancey, *The Jesus I Never Knew* (Grand Rapids, MI: Zondervan, 1995), 88.

Mark 1:40–42 provides one of my favorite stories about the life of Christ. In this passage, Jesus encounters a leper. We are quite fortunate today that leprosy has been all but eradicated, at least in the United States. But in Jesus's day, leprosy was a death sentence, both physically and relationally. Lepers could not be a part of society for two reasons. First, they were ceremonially unclean. This meant they were not permitted in the temple and could not worship with everyone else. They were outcasts. Further, if a person came in close contact with a leper, that person also became unclean. So, lepers were shunned. And second, the disease of leprosy is highly contagious. No one wanted to be around a leper for fear that they would become infected. Certainly, no one would touch a leper. Can you imagine what the life of the leper in this biblical account would have been like? He was an outcast. Society despised and rejected this man. He was unwelcome. How long must it have been since the last time the leper experienced the touch of another human being, let alone a meaningful hug?

I am sure Jesus Christ thought about all these things, and it moved Him. He was able and willing to feel compassion for others. And His compassion moved Him not only to heal this man but to heal him by touching him! This is important because Jesus healed lots of people by simply speaking. But this man, Jesus touched! As the leper knelt down, hoping simply to be recognized, I like to envision Jesus reaching out His arm and shocking him with a touch. Maybe Jesus even gave the man a much-needed hug.

Jesus Shared Anger

Some of us believe the feeling of anger is somehow bad. However, anger is something we all feel. More than that, anger is the exact right feeling for some situations. When I hear a story of someone being abused, I am filled with anger, and rightfully so. The problem for many of us is not in the feeling of anger, but in what we do with that feeling. Often, we make one of two mistakes. Either we suppress the anger and don't share with others how and why we are angry, or we act improperly out of that anger. Both mistakes often end up hurting us and others.

In Mark 3:3-5, we read of Jesus experiencing two different feelings—anger and grief. Both are appropriate. In this story, Jesus encounters a man with a "withered hand." Instead of bringing the man to Jesus for healing, the religious leaders of the day sat and watched to see if they could trap Jesus into breaking a commandment because it was the Sabbath, when they were to do no work. They believed that even healing was work that shouldn't occur on the Sabbath. That those who should care the most about people who were suffering cared more about trapping Jesus or following certain laws rather than helping this hurting man really angered Jesus. It should anger us as well. Jesus recognized what was going on, and it influenced Him. Here's how Mark records it: "And he [Jesus] said to the man with the withered hand, 'Come here.' And he said to them [the religious leaders], 'Is it lawful on the Sabbath to do good or to do harm, to save life or to kill?' But they were silent. And he looked around at them with anger, grieved at their hardness of heart, and said to the man, 'Stretch out your hand.' He stretched it out, and his hand was restored." If it was right for Jesus to feel anger, why wouldn't it—in certain situations—be right for us?

Jesus Shared Indignation

All of us, from time to time, see or experience things that are simply not fair. These things might anger us, as they angered Jesus. They might also lead us to feel indignant, just as they did Christ. Indignation is very similar to anger, but differs in that indignation carries with it a type of annoyance that often leads to action. Mark 10:13–16 shares a famous account of Jesus telling His disciples that the kingdom of God belongs to those who receive it "like a child." Mark's account describes Jesus and His feelings and actions related to those who would prevent children from coming to Him: "And they were bringing children to him that he might touch them, and the disciples rebuked them. But when Jesus saw it, he was indignant and said to them, 'Let the children come to me; do not hinder them, for to such belongs the kingdom of God. Truly, I say to you, whoever does not receive the kingdom of God like a child shall not enter it.' And he took them in his arms and blessed them, laying his hands on them."

Jesus Shared Zeal

Zeal and enthusiasm are important. These two closely related feelings often stem directly from passion. I'm grateful God gives us appropriate passions and allows us to share those passions with others. Never forget, the Lord Jesus was full of passion and had a zeal for the right things. When Jesus cleansed the temple during Passover as recorded in John 2:13–17, "His disciples remembered that it was written, 'Zeal for your house will consume me.'" Do we ever think about Jesus with the sense that any feeling consumed Him?

Jesus Shared That He Could Be Deeply Moved

There is a Greek word *embrimaomai*, which in John 11:33 is translated as "deeply moved" or "deeply angered." The word has the connotation of snorting with anger like a horse. Have you ever seen an angry horse? A horse that is agitated or uncomfortable? Now, can you imagine Jesus looking or acting like that? The disciples witnessed it.

Jesus loved deeply, cared deeply, and allowed Himself to be moved deeply on behalf of others. We see a good example of this after His good friend Lazarus died. Jesus arrived four days after His friend's passing to meet Lazarus's sisters, Mary and Martha, who were also dear friends of Jesus. Even though Jesus knew what He planned to do, and that Lazarus would rise from the dead, Jesus allowed Himself to feel the weight of loss and hurt along with His friends. He was grieving for these dear people. Grief is yet another important feeling Jesus shared with His followers. As He saw the pain in all who were there, He almost certainly was also angry about the fact that sin caused all this pain.

We learn this about Jesus from what happened next. "When Jesus saw her [Mary] weeping, and the Jews who had come with her also weeping, he was *deeply moved in his spirit and greatly troubled*" (italics mine). This verse clearly states that those who were there knew unequivocally that Jesus was feeling alongside them. He was emotional, hurting, and angered to the point that John chose the word *embrimaomai* to describe it. And, in case we might think this was a one-off for Jesus, a few verses later, John declares in 11:38: "Then Jesus, deeply moved again, came to the tomb. It was a cave, and a stone lay against it."

Jesus Shared That He Could Be Brought to Tears

The single shortest verse in all the Bible is John 11:35: "Jesus wept." After being deeply moved in His spirit and asking to see where Lazarus had been buried, we see our Lord weeping with those He loved. Jesus was not only willing to empathize and feel with His friends, He allowed Himself to be seen and known in His hurt. Jesus did not hide His feelings. He wept for all to see. As I said, for no good reason, people today deem it a sign of weakness for men to cry. Nothing could be further from the truth. Tears can be a very healthy and helpful thing. When we cry with another human being, they know we really care, really feel, and really love. Consider the outcome of Jesus and His crying: "So the Jews said, 'See how he loved him!'" (John 11:36).

Jesus Shared His Joy

Lest we think Jesus was always sad or angry, we should also realize He was described in Matthew 11:19 and Luke 7:34 as a friend of sinners. Most people do not gravitate toward someone who is constantly sad or angry. Jesus shared every shade of feeling. He was also full of love and joy. In fact, He was and is the embodiment of both. Jesus often felt joy and shared His joyousness with those around Him. I can't help but wonder if that is not part of the reason why so many people who wanted nothing to do with the religion of that time wanted to be with Jesus. This account from Luke 10:21 shares Luke's recollection of one instance of Jesus visibly and verbally sharing the joy He felt: "In that same hour he [Jesus] rejoiced in the Holy Spirit."

So, if Jesus, being fully a man, could feel and share those feelings, we can as well. It makes no difference whether we are male or female. Not only that, but if we are Christian, it should mean that we are Christlike or, at a minimum, becoming more Christlike. As the apostle Paul declared to the church at Corinth in 2 Corinthians 3:18, "we all, with unveiled face, beholding the glory of the Lord, are being transformed into the same image from one degree of glory to another." If we are truly being transformed to look more and more like Christ, it seems natural to me to think we should be ever increasing in our expression of joy. When this occurs and we become more like Christ, we will naturally have intimacy in our relationships. Using our feelings is central to just how much intimacy you and I will have with others.

As I shared earlier, the intimacy I have with God today certainly involved my willingness to be truthful and stop hiding from Him. It absolutely required me to allow myself to be known by God and to seek to know Him. However, a big part of both things involved the use and sharing of my feelings. I can say unequivocally that my relationship with both God and others would not be what it is today apart from the use of my feelings.

NEXT STEPS

I have two next steps for you in this chapter. First, consider how often you allow yourself to simply feel. Do you give yourself the time? Is allowing yourself to feel and process those feelings, as well as sharing those feelings with others, important to you? How much better could you be as a friend, coworker, spouse, parent, or child if you regularly allowed yourself to feel alongside others? And second, how are you doing at sharing your feelings? How many feeling words do you know? Consider doing a Google search on "feeling words" or buying a book on sharing your feelings. Like most other things, this is an area we all can improve on. It simply takes focus and effort.

CHAPTER 9

Why Don't We Feel?

We just examined the importance of feeling in building a healthy life and relational intimacy. It's an easy truth to accept, but why don't we do it? Why do we struggle with allowing ourselves to feel deeply in the first place? Further, what makes it so difficult to share those feelings with others? There are many factors, but I believe seven significant reasons are behind most people's unwillingness to feel or to share their feelings.

After we explore each of these reasons and consider how we might get past them, we will look specifically at how feeling and then sharing those feelings fuels intimacy. I want to encourage us to not simply face and understand the things holding us back, but to come away with an excitement for what the future will look like when we become more adept at sharing feelings. Let's begin, though, with the things holding us back and consider ways to move beyond them.

We Are Scared

Sharing our feelings can be scary. Rejection is a possibility any time we share our real feelings. People could laugh at us or misunderstand us. We might share our feelings the wrong way and cause hurt or embarrassment. In addition, because we have not learned how to share our feelings, we often feel as if we don't know how to. Fear is one of the most powerful motivators on the planet, and, unfortunately, fear can keep us from doing things we know would ultimately benefit us. It's natural for us to feel a certain amount of fear regarding sharing our feelings.

When I first made a commitment to share my feelings, it was a behavior so foreign it felt bizarre. I really was afraid. It seems weird to admit I didn't know how to feel, but that is close to the truth. I found a vast range of emotions when I first allowed myself to feel. I assumed others would not understand my feelings, would feel differently than I did, or would outright reject me or my feelings. But I soon realized that, many times, those with whom I interacted had more understanding of and compassion for my feelings than practically anything else.

For example, nine years ago I didn't think any of my friends would understand my feelings of pure disgust at the thought of being close to my mom after all the things she'd done to me. Instead, I discovered that those who cared also empathized and hurt with me, even if they couldn't relate, having never experienced abuse like that firsthand. One of the reasons I think we do receive compassion and understanding is that our feelings are common among our peers. Knowing that everyone feels and has similar feelings about a wide range of subjects both freed me and encouraged me.

And yet, while it's one thing to discover that I can share and not be rejected, it's completely another thing to verbalize how I feel with no track record to go on. Here's what I found. At some point, I simply needed to begin. It's much like the first several times I dove after becoming scuba certified. It was scary, but I knew there was a lot of beauty to be experienced if I allowed myself to do it. After a while, diving became second nature. My fear subsided and excitement became the norm. A similar process took over once I began sharing my feelings. There was a natural excitement that built in expecting others close to me to connect with me through those feelings.

The World Teaches Us Not to Share Our Feelings

Let's face it, the world basically tells us it's fine to have feelings, but we should keep them to ourselves. By our actions alone, we often communicate to others that we don't desire to hear their feelings, don't have time to hear their feelings, and don't care one way or another whether we hear their feelings. Worse, most of us have had a negative experience in which we took the risk of sharing our feelings, only to be rejected or made to feel stupid for feeling the way we did. These are ways the world's system tells us, "Don't share your feelings!"

The only way around this, for me, is threefold. First, I continually remind myself not to listen to the world, because the world and most others do not have my best interest at heart. Second, it is always important for me to remember who I should be listening to. As a Christian, I'm called to listen to Christ and the lessons of His teaching. It shouldn't matter what the world says. It matters what God says. Finally, I know I have people who do care about me, and these people are interested in my feelings.

It Hurts

Sharing our feelings requires us to first connect with our feelings. To put our feelings into words requires us to think about them. This can be difficult for those of us who are not good at formulating our thoughts or words. It requires extra thought and processing. For negative or painful feelings, the process of identifying our feelings can hurt to the point of tears. Most of us will do anything to avoid pain, and certainly hiding our feelings seems like a much easier and less painful approach than sharing them.

While everything I just shared is true, I did not consider for many years how much pain and hurt also happened when I buried my feelings. However, there is a significant difference between dealing with pain and hurt alone and allowing others to share it with us. Plus, when I hide my feelings, I do not receive the benefit of experiencing love and acceptance from others.

We Don't Trust Another Person Enough

Often, whether we choose to share our feelings with another human being is based on how much we trust that person. Sharing our feelings requires vulnerability, and we frequently believe most people have not earned the right to be trusted with our vulnerability. We do not want to give up control and don't want to risk being hurt. Ultimately, what we are really saying is this: I don't trust this person to respond to my feelings appropriately.

We Incorrectly Believe Sharing Feelings Is a Sign of Weakness or Don't See the Value in It

Whether we're male or female, society wrongly teaches that we are weak when we share our feelings, especially if they are accompanied by tears. Our employers typically expect us to work with minimal expression of our feelings. The motto goes something like this: Get the job done. Anything that takes us away from the job, like taking time to feel, hurts the bottom line. Sadly, many times, we take this attitude home with us. People today are so busy that if I were to ask you to take fifteen minutes every day to share with another human being how you are feeling, you would probably tell me you don't have the time. Is it that we really do not have the time, or is it that we don't see the value? Either way, we are saying that expressing our feelings is "wasted time," at least in relation to all the other things we could be doing. The Gospel account of Matthew records Jesus saying in Matthew 6:21: "For where your treasure is, there your heart will be also." One of the most treasured things for every human is our time. All of us, regardless of our wealth or status, get the same twenty-four hours every day. We give our time to the things we value. Many of us don't share our feelings because we simply don't see the value in it enough to spend the time.

I had to learn early in my pursuit of intimacy that my priorities with regard to time were completely out of whack. I realized I had wasted a lot of time on a lot of foolish things. As I grew during my intimacy journey, I learned to prioritize things that are important, and that sharing my feelings with others was something I could indeed control and could choose to do. I've since learned that sharing with others might be the very best use of any minute of the day.

It Goes Against How We Were Raised

When I first wrote this chapter, I was at the same time preparing to speak at a parenting conference where I was to present a breakout session. The hope was that my presentation would help parents become the best parents they could be. I now know how important it is that children both see intimacy modeled with them and have it taught to them. Plus, I know very few parents talk about intimacy with their kids. While this is problematic, there is another reality in many families that is equally troubling: many parents raise their kids to be disconnected from their feelings. Parents do not teach their kids that it's okay to feel whatever they feel. Most parents don't teach their children that their feelings are a part of their magnificent bodies, created uniquely by God. God wants to hear those feelings, and so should we. My parents almost never asked how I was feeling unless it was to determine whether I had a medical illness. How about you? Were you encouraged to think about how you were feeling and why? Did your mom or dad sit and listen to the things in your heart? Were your feelings and thoughts valued at home? I've talked to very few people for whom this was true. We most commonly practice the things we learned by watching our parents and siblings.

This point is hard for me to write about because it is an area where I, too, failed my kids. To this day, I don't do as good a job as I should in simply sitting with them and listening to their feelings. I know I need to improve in this area. My kids and your kids are worth it.

Sharing Feelings Is Not Modeled at Home, at Work, or at Church

Like our children, we don't stay at home forever (at least our parents hope we don't). We move on as grown adults to lives of work. At work, coworkers are encouraged to work together for the common good. Yet this rarely involves the regular exchange of feelings. For many employees, their bosses rarely care how they feel about something. The expectation is that the job gets done. It would not surprise me if well over half of the people reading this have heard something like "just get it done" in their careers. Even if we're not verbally discouraged by our bosses, why would we naturally begin sharing our feelings in the workplace if we haven't customarily done that at home or at school?

And it's not just that we don't share our feelings in those situations. We're not encouraged to share them at church either. As we've seen already, Jesus regularly shared His feelings with His followers. However, I expect in virtually every church, the opposite is modeled every single Sunday. In fact, I was recently at a safety conference for business leaders where the officer leading the conference introduced the term "church greeting syndrome." Church greeting syndrome, he explained, is what happens almost every week at church. Congregants walk in and hear something to the effect of "Hey, how are you doing?" The response from 99 percent of people is something on the order of "I'm good, how are you?" Some might dress up their reply with something that sounds more righteous, like "Better than I deserve. How about you?"

But think about it. Even if we drop our percentage to, say, 85 percent responding that way, are 85 percent of people really doing "good" or even "okay" every week? I can tell you, the answer is no. Likely, a majority of people are not. Many individuals you see at church on Sunday had a terrible week. Some are on the verge of losing everything. For some, it took everything to get dressed and come to church. Nevertheless, it's modeled week after week, from the church leadership down to the individual church members, that we never really share what is going on in our own lives— we never share our feelings. Rather, we do the "church thing" and act with everyone else like we have it all together. We don't dare allow others to see that we have feelings of hurt, brokenness, and other negative real-life emotions that we bring with us every Sunday.

Moving Beyond
Our Hindrances

If you and I could honestly deal with each of those obstacles that can hold us back from feeling and sharing our feelings with others, what would be the benefits beyond what we looked at in the last chapter? What is it about sharing our feelings that is so important? What impact does it have either way on intimacy? Let's consider the answer to each of these reasonable questions and consider further how allowing ourselves to feel and share those feelings fuels intimacy. There are at least five realities that occur whenever we practice this behavior. Each of these realities opens our relationships to becoming more intimate.

We Share Truth

Other than God's Word, I cannot think of anything truer than our feelings. I'm not saying our feelings are right or wrong. I'm saying they are true and natural. You can try to make yourself feel a certain way, but things will always happen that make you feel one way or another. When I see a mother with a newborn baby, full of love and happiness, I feel joy. In the right situation, it can bring tears to my eyes. That joy is genuine. I don't have to compel it. It is just there. Much the same way, when I am with someone who has just lost a loved one, I often have feelings of grief and loss. These feelings are natural and true. They are real and convey truth about who we are and where we are, emotionally and spiritually. As we looked at in chapter four, truth is always at the center of intimacy. The more two human beings can share truth with each other, the tighter and more intimate a relationship between them becomes. Sharing feelings is simply another way to be more true, thus also more intimate.

As I mentioned earlier, I recently attended my grandmother's celebration of life service. In this service, a very important thing happened. I mourned, grieved, and cried with many other caring people. The love of my grandma connected us together. In our communal sharing, whether we knew it or not, we were loving each other. I had never met some of the people at this service before. Yet all of us became a bit more intimate with each other because of the truth we shared that day.

We Open Ourselves Up to Either Being Accepted or Being Rejected

Whenever someone openly shares their feelings, they become vulnerable. We never can know for certain exactly how others will react to our feelings. Will they understand and feel the same way? What if they feel completely the opposite? When I open myself up, I'm looking for a connection, but what if that's not what I get? Vulnerability may be one of the biggest keys that unlock intimacy, because every time we are vulnerable and receive another's acceptance and care, we become closer to that individual. We know we are being loved. As I stated earlier, intimacy is not possible without both parties having a willingness to be vulnerable. There might not be a better way to be vulnerable than to share our feelings frequently with those we care about.

We Allow Ourselves to Really Connect with Another Person

I cannot stress enough the importance of empathy in relationships. This is true of relationships at every level. The world is so often missing empathy. Worse yet, most people mistake empathy for sympathy. The two are not synonymous. Earlier in the book, I shared a brief excerpt from *Saving Your Marriage before It Starts*. Authors Les and Leslie Parrott do a marvelous job of helping us understand both the importance of empathy and the simple difference between it and sympathy. Here are some of their insights:

> Empathy is perhaps the toughest work of building a strong marriage. Because most of us are wired to use either our head or heart, one more than the other, it takes a conscious effort to empathize. In Les's book *Love's Unseen Enemy*, he describes how loving with our heart alone is only sympathizing, while loving with our head alone is simply analyzing. Empathy, however, brings together both sympathetic and analytic abilities, both heart and head, to fully

understand our partners. Empathy says, "If I were you, I would act as you do; I understand why you feel the way you feel."

Empathy always involves risk, so be forewarned. Accurately understanding your partner's hurts and hopes will change you—but the benefits of taking that risk far outweigh the disadvantages.[25]

While the Parrotts were writing for those pursuing a happy marriage, their statements really apply to all relationships we hope to experience as intimate. When we are empathetic in a relationship, we really move a relationship to a different level. It creates tight bonds that are not easily broken and thus really does fuel intimacy. No, it's not easy. Yes, it can be painful. And yes, it is a skill and practice we can learn and grow in.

I wasn't always great at being empathetic. I could be sympathetic with the best of them, but I could not share empathy because I wouldn't allow myself to feel. At some point, I realized I had to change. I'll never forget an experience that occurred about two years into recovery, when I had an opportunity to practice deeper empathy with my wife. Tammy had returned from a women's conference she had attended with several women from our church. I asked what I thought would be a simple question: "How did the conference go?" Her answer showed that she trusted me and was willing to be vulnerable, and it gave me the opportunity to empathetically connect with her feelings, despite my wrongs.

---

[25]   Les Parrott and Leslie Parrott, *Saving Your Marriage before It Starts* (Grand Rapids, MI: Zondervan, 2006), 86.

Tammy told me that during a break at the conference, she had walked through the conference hall where the attendees could visit various vendors' tables. At one such table was a book on how to improve Christian sex life. When Tammy saw this, she was immediately reminded of my past sin and how I had made a mockery of Christian sex life in our marriage. Relating her story, she wept as she told me that all she could do was cry as she walked away from that vendor's table. What probably was an opportunity for many women to purchase something that could be a help to them became a trigger for my bride, who simply was a victim of the sins of her husband.

As my wife told me this, I revisited how I had severely wronged her. I cried myself as I thought about how painful it must have been to be her in that situation. I could feel her hurt. I sought to imagine being in her shoes. I also thought of how my actions had caused her so much pain and still were doing so. I thought briefly about how others had victimized me and how angry that made me. Except now, I directed my anger at myself for hurting my lovely wife. As we cried, I thanked her for revealing that to me. I told her again that I was sorry. And I promised to always love and support her, which meant hearing from her any time she needed to open up about how I had hurt her.

I'd like to report that the rest of our day was great. It wasn't. Nevertheless, the experience drew us much closer together. It fueled both connection and intimacy. My wife's feelings were heard, accepted, and validated. She was loved. And I became even more adamant about making sure she would never be hurt this way again. Had both of us not been able and willing to share our feelings with each other, we both would have missed out on this opportunity to connect and grow in intimacy.

We Honestly Admit Our Lack of Control

Most of us, if we're honest, can admit to times when the tears came, we had no idea where they were coming from, and yet we couldn't stop them. One time I was sitting in a church service after my mother passed away. Remember, she abused me in so many ways I wanted nothing to do with her. The thought of her and her abuse disgusted me. It still does. Sitting in church that day, I cried. I didn't know why I was crying. Looking back on it now, I believe I was crying over what I had missed in a mother. I may have been crying over the hope I once had, which now was finally and permanently gone. Here's what I can tell you for certain: I could not control my tears.

In much the same way that I couldn't control my tears that day, I can't control my feelings on any day. Our feelings are what they are. They come to us, and then we must work with and process them. I have learned now how to process them through all kinds of lenses. I have knowledge and experience that may well instruct me to feel differently. But when I share my feelings with others, I'm admitting that this is how whatever I'm experiencing or going through in life is hitting me at the moment. And I really don't have control over how I feel. Most of us don't want to admit to ourselves that we don't have control over our feelings or life itself. We certainly don't want to share with others that we don't have control. But this is one more way to allow others to empathize with us. Others can join us by saying, "It's okay. I care. I'm with you. You don't have to be in control of your feelings or this situation." Realizing we don't have to be in control all the time and learning to trust others strengthens the intimacy we share.

We Become Free

So many people regrettably never experience the freedom of being really known. Many have deep feelings about a vast number of things they have never told others for a variety of reasons. Most people in this situation don't realize they are hiding. Back in chapter one, I mentioned the children's game hide-and-seek. Thinking about that game, how well would it go for a person who is hiding to run around, making himself loud and visible? Not well, right? He'd be found. The inverse is true about us and our feelings. When we lock up our feelings and don't make them loud and visible, we are closing ourselves off and, essentially, are not allowing ourselves to be found. But it's worse than that. Often, we not only keep ourselves from being found, but we reinforce invisible cages that trap us. But when we allow others to know us completely, regularly sharing our feelings, we open our cage doors, which lead to freedom.

There is an amazing freedom that comes from being real. It is truly exciting to be in relationships where I am known and accepted. This includes others knowing and accepting me with all my feelings. We will never be truly free if there are feelings we believe we must restrain and keep from others. I dare say, intimacy fully depends on freedom. Thankfully, it is cyclical. Intimacy also produces more freedom.

So, if we want to experience relationships marked by intimacy, we have to learn to feel and learn to share those feelings with others. Day by day, we need to make the hard choice to become vulnerable and allow others to empathize with us. True, they may not empathize with us, and that could be painful. Despite that prospect, we need to realize that feeling the emotional and physical touch of others has a lasting, positive impact on us and on them. The possible hurt and rejection is worth the risk. We can do it. We must do it.

NEXT STEP

Your next step for this chapter is to pinpoint the primary obstacle holding you back from regularly sharing your feelings. Once you've determined that, set a correction plan to start working on it. The more you share your feelings, the easier it becomes. Could you schedule five minutes every day to intentionally share your feelings with someone else? If that seems too long, how about three minutes before your lunch break? You can do it!

CHAPTER 10

Buy Another's Chairs

About six years ago, my wife paid me one of the greatest compliments I've received from her in quite some time amid a conversation we were having with a friend about how we were doing. The individual we were talking to knows our story, and he knew at the time that we were both pursuing real intimacy with each other. I was finally being transparent and real with my wife on a regular basis. Tammy was learning to trust the real Rob. In that setting and in answer to a direct question about how we were doing, my wife responded that we were doing pretty well. When asked to elaborate on the change that had occurred and why we were doing well, Tammy said this: "Rob is buying my chairs."

Because you may be as lost as the friend we were talking with, let me explain. Tammy's comment about "buying chairs" was a reference to the 1996 film *Phenomenon*,[26] in which the main character shows his love for a woman by secretly purchasing the chairs she delights in building but can't seem to sell. With this metaphor, Tammy meant that I was now paying attention to the things that were important to her and investing in them. It so happens that my wife, through her abundant creative ability, loves to buy beat-up old furniture, including chairs, and then refinish and sell her creations. But Tammy wasn't saying that I was literally spending my money on her remade furniture. She was communicating that after all our years together, I was finally paying attention to her dreams and passions, and actively supporting her in them.

Buying someone's chairs begins with finding out what another person puts his or her heart into. We all have chairs, and we need others to buy those chairs. We all have passions, desires, wants, needs, cravings, interests, and things that make us unique and individual. But we often do a miserable job of finding out what each other's chairs are. The compliment Tammy gave me to our friend was that, for once, I really was considering what Tammy cared about and investing in those things. I really cared about her passions and was willing to give of my time and effort to support her. Doing so was a central part of our growing in intimacy.

---

[26]   *Phenomenon*, directed by Jon Turteltaub (Touchstone Pictures, 1996).

I've thought about her compliment often since then. Usually, my thoughts begin with regret. I regret the many years of my life when I was so self-centered, rarely making time to honestly pursue my wife. I regret how much time I missed being truly intimate, time I missed truly knowing my wife in a way that would have been intensely meaningful to us both. Tammy lived the first twenty years of our marriage not knowing every moment that her husband was her biggest fan and supporter. More often than not, her chairs were piling up, waiting to be purchased.

Fortunately, though, my thoughts these days don't stay mired in regret. Today, I am buying her chairs, or at least I am making an earnest effort to do so. This has led to wonderful new thoughts, emotions, and experiences I never would have believed could happen.

For example, I'm learning that I like my wife's chairs a lot! One of her chairs is her creative ability. Tammy finds beat-up old furniture that most people (or I, at least) couldn't care less about. She sees this furniture for what it could be and looks to put her creative touches on it. She might refinish it using colorful paint, or she might use a stain that brings out some remarkable feature of the original wood grain. She might paint by hand a picture to create a custom bench or add just the perfect text to make a piece of furniture become something more artful. Frankly, I see it now as a reflection of what God does, and I love it.

Buying her chairs has meant that now I see things I didn't before. It invites me to be a part of what she does and who she is. While I am limited in my creative ability, I can look for furniture for her. Rarely do I succeed. However, I'm connecting with her. As I connect with her in this way, I experience joy. It is fun stretching myself beyond what I would otherwise do on my own. Even writing this section of the chapter is putting a smile on my face, knowing how much I enjoy connecting with my wife and encouraging her as she pursues her passions. I now realize how much more full life is when each of us buys each other's chairs. I'm learning, too, just how important buying each other's chairs is to intimacy.

Along those lines, I'm also realizing that buying each other's chairs applies not only in marriage relationships, but in every relationship to be marked by intimacy. If I want to develop intimacy with another human being, that person is going to need to buy my chairs, and I'm going to need to buy theirs. What does this mean and what does it look like? To answer those questions, I've identified four central truths related to buying chairs.

Truth One: You Can't Buy Chairs If You're Broke

One of my weaknesses is that I'm terrible with money. I don't budget well and, I have to admit, have spent most of my life living beyond my means. I received a credit card from a bank *way* too early in my life and began my financial adulthood in debt. Unfortunately, I learned I can purchase many things on credit and, provided I still have room in my limit, pay for dinner, trips, household items, and even some bills using a credit card.

I've figured out, though, you can't buy another person's chairs on credit. There are no emotional credit cards. Coming to terms with this reality usually leads us to a couple of important points. Each point requires some additional thought and build-out. First, there is an actuality we rarely think about or possibly even admit. There is an actual cost to buying another person's chairs. Second, and while this may seem to go without saying, if there is a cost, then there is also some currency to pay for that cost. It would be wise to think about these subjects now.

In addition, it's worth noting that it is much simpler and costs nothing to *not* invest in another person and their chairs. Nothing, that is, except intimacy. Far more often than not, people consciously or subconsciously decide not to pay the costs. Of all the reasons, one of the top ones may simply be that we know we don't have the right currency. Or we don't want to commit to spending it.

So, what are the costs of buying another's chairs?

There is a cost to pay to buy another person's chairs, but it isn't money. Instead, the costs are related more to who we are and what we can give of ourselves. As I've grown in my understanding of intimacy in relationships, I've realized that all of us are works in progress. All of us can grow, and many of us really need to grow significantly if we want the most out of our relationships. Nine years ago, I was close to bankrupt as a person. Yes, I was financially poor, but I also was poor in my understanding and ability to do what was needed in relationships to have them defined by intimacy. I didn't stay that way. I learned and I changed. The sections that follow describe some of the various types of currency that I discovered are prerequisites for buying another's chairs.

Time

It takes time to learn, understand, comprehend, discuss, and pursue another person and their chairs. Ask any marriage counselor what he or she hears as a common problem in hurting marriages and the answer will be that the husband and wife do not spend quality time with each other. They don't date. They don't have meaningful conversations. Couples in troubled marriages do not make the choice to invest time in each other. Frankly, we're often so inwardly focused that we can be selfish with our time. We are unwilling to invest the time necessary to buy another's chairs. You can never purchase another person's chairs without making time to do so.

But it's not just time we must pay. It's quality time. I don't know about you, but I can be really scatter-brained and unable to focus. When it comes to spending time together, what people really want from others is quality time. They want focused time, given with intentionality. It's about saying in a practical sense, "I'm giving you, and you alone, my time, my undivided attention, because you are that important to me."

When we do this, we are communicating that another person and the things they are passionate about are important enough for us to give up something as precious as our time. The inverse of this is also true. When we use our time on everything but supporting the passions and interests of those we say we care about, we essentially are communicating that they aren't worth it—and this always comes at the cost of an intimate relationship.

There's one last item I'd like to encourage us to think about as it relates to time. Everyone sees the value in time. God gives every person only twenty-four hours in a day. Many of us give our time when it's convenient. When people have plenty of free time and they make some of that available, does it have the same value as when a person who is extremely busy carves out the time? Of course not. I've found that leftovers might be great for pot roast, but they're terrible for developing intimate relationships.

Commitment and Faithfulness

Unlike purchases made at department stores, there is no returning the purchase of another's chairs. If you make the investment, you have made the investment and can't take it back. You wouldn't want to take it back anyway, but when you think about costs, consider that you only have so many resources available. Once you expend those resources, you won't have those same resources for other necessary or desired wants. For example, if I spend time with anyone or on anything, that time is now gone, and I can't regain it. I assure you, when looking back on my life, I wish I had used my time better.

In addition, commitment often requires more than just time. It may mean sacrifice, including giving up things you want. Even though I said it doesn't cost money to buy a person's chairs, you may incur some financial costs if you are investing in another's passion. (Tammy needs to buy her paint.) Understand, when you choose to buy another's chairs, you are making a commitment, or else you really aren't buying their chairs. I find that people are often great at admiring other people's chairs without making the commitment to buy them.

Now, many people are great at making commitments and have no problem doing so. Where some of these people lack is in their follow-through. Some simply are not faithful people. Their yes doesn't really mean yes; it means maybe. In order for us to pay the cost of buying another's chairs, we have to be trustworthy.

I hate to admit it, but for many years of my life I was not all that trustworthy. I was broken in this area. Tammy, in many ways, couldn't really trust me. I had proven time and again that I was good at saying something and not following through. A big part of the growth in our intimacy occurred as a result of my becoming trustworthy and faithful. Indeed, it's possible that when Tammy said I was buying her chairs, she meant I not only gave lip service to her passions and interests but followed up what I said with what I did.

A Willingness and Ability to Feel

This may sound strange, but an investment in another person's chairs requires deep feeling. It requires the use of our emotions, including emotions we sometimes don't like to use. Many of us, if we're honest, don't want to do this. As I've mentioned, we are unwilling to open ourselves up and become vulnerable. Feeling can be hard and messy, and who wants to sign up to experience sadness, pain, anxiety, fear, and other tough stuff, especially in front of others? However, this really is a true cost of buying another's chairs.

Let me use my wife and her creativity with furniture as a quick example. What happens if Tammy creates something, and others don't like it? Frankly, what if I don't like it? What would it mean to have an honest dialogue about that? What if people don't purchase the items that Tammy works on? How will she feel? Am I willing to sit with her in her sadness? For me to pursue Tammy's chairs, I may need to feel feelings of my own personal inadequacy and inability.

Emotional Capacity

If there is any area aside from having and making quality time where people are unprepared to buy another's chairs, it's likely that they don't have the emotional capacity to do so. Many, many people today live life emotionally and spiritually bankrupt. These people have deep wounds from their life experience that they have never dealt with. The result is that they cannot truly and correctly empathize and feel because they are not allowing themselves to feel for themselves first.

I can say unequivocally that this was true for me for much of my adult life. As I stated earlier, until eight to nine years ago, I hadn't properly worked through my upbringing and the abuse I suffered as a young man. There was part of my inmost being that was crying out, desiring to be heard, but never truly allowed to do so. I emotionally could not be fully intimate with another person because I was never fully available to another person. A requirement for me to invest in another person emotionally was to learn to feel things myself—good things and bad things. Emotional capacity means that we can allow ourselves to feel hurt, pain, fear, love, and forgiveness, along with many other feelings.

So, to summarize Truth One, no credit is available to purchase another's chairs, and you can't do so with an empty wallet. If you've struggled with intimacy and connecting with another human being, I challenge you to examine yourself more carefully. Are you capable of having intimate relationships? If not, choose right now to change that. Become a person committed to investing in other people and begin experiencing a new sense of joy, possibly more than you ever have before. If you're prepared and are ready to invest, let's move on to Truth Two.

Truth Two: You Must Go Shopping

Some people love it, but I hate to shop. Crowds and stores (especially the combination) bother me.

I'm perfectly happy sitting on a bench in a mall while Tammy gets what she wants or what we need. Ultimately, I've learned that it's better for me to tag along and attempt to be a part of this experience than to communicate through my actions that Tammy is alone when seeking to satisfy her shopping itch. It means something to my wife when I commit to going and being with her.

While I hate literal shopping, fortunately that kind of shopping is not what I'm talking about in Truth Two. To metaphorically buy another's chairs, you aren't likely to have to visit any store—although going along on those shopping trips might still be a wise move. That's because the skills (yes, there are skills) and decisions required when shopping are necessary if you're going to buy another's chairs. In relationships, there are at least four skills or decisions that must be considered and learned that mirror actual shopping.

1. **You must have desire.** Without desire, nothing ever happens by choice. There are many things pulling at us for our attention. This is life. Before you can buy another's chairs, the person who owns the chairs must know you desire to buy them. This is important: what you say and what you do are two different things. Desire is not so much a "said" thing as it is a "done" thing. Others will properly discern your desire, or lack thereof, far more by what you do than by what you say. (However, note: what you say is important as well.)

2. **You must commit the time.** In the days before
    the internet, one could spend hours searching
    for something, a task that now takes ten
    minutes (if that) on the computer with a few
    clicks. Even so, there are still some things,
    like works of art and fine jewelry, that require
    time spent. When shopping for another's
    chairs, a good search engine might help you
    do some research, but it probably will not do
    much to reduce the time you need to commit.
    I'll abbreviate this point because I've already
    shared so much about time in Truth One.
    But it is always important to recognize and
    remember that your relationship and intimacy
    don't just take time at the beginning. Both
    continue to require quality time as they grow.

3. **Focus is essential.** I think most men are
    terrible at paying attention. In my opinion,
    guys seem so easily distracted. I know
    when my wife and I go out to dinner, I have
    to intentionally sit where there are no
    television screens in my line of sight if I'm
    going to stay focused on her throughout
    our meal. This is really sad, because my
    sweet wife is beautiful. But my eyes can
    easily wander to the football game or other
    sporting event being broadcast from the
    bar behind her. I'm purposefully deciding
    to focus my attention where it belongs—on
    Tammy.

Focus is equally important in shopping for another person's chairs. Otherwise, it's easy to get distracted and miss seeing what we want to buy. Have you ever been shopping with someone who went to the store intending to purchase one item but became so distracted that they purchased several other items and left without buying what they originally came for? I believe the same thing occurs all the time with relation to another's chairs. We have to focus our attention on the other person. What makes her glow? What makes him excited? Does she talk about anything specific? What are her deepest longings? Are there unrealized dreams still out there? What has he accomplished that he's really proud of? Are there clues about a person's interests you have overlooked? These are just a few questions we might ask to focus our attention. Doing so is essential in buying another's chairs.

4. **You must pay attention to detail.** Though you may see this observation as an elaboration on the subject of focus, it is different. While focus points our attention in the right direction, attention to detail examines closely what truly is important. Think about it like this: Scientists looking for microorganisms or other tiny things that are invisible to the naked eye begin

with a microscope and a slide. Focus is really moving the slide into the correct position and adjusting the lenses so the scientist can clearly see what he or she is looking at. Attention to detail is the key to what comes next, as the scientist closely observes characteristics to discern what's on that slide and distinguish one object from another. In much the same way, if you are going to buy another's chairs, you need to not only fine-tune your vision and hearing, but apply them acutely to the specifics of your loved one's passions. Think for a moment about the actual chairs we sit in. Consider the vast number of shapes, styles, wood types, coverings, colors, fabrics, patterns, and functions that exist in something as simple as a chair. The same is true of every person's passions, interests, desires, wants, dreams, and so on. Are you willing to take the time necessary to pay close enough attention to find out the exact type of chair you need to buy that is specific to your partner? If you are going to shop properly, you must become a student of detail. Doing so will pay huge dividends and make shopping much easier.

Truth Three: Styles and Patterns Change

Truth Three in our list of chair-buying essentials deals with the reality of change. If there is one constant in life, it is that things change. In 1998, Spencer Johnson published his book *Who Moved My Cheese?*[27] The overall concept, in case you haven't read it, is that we are like mice in a maze, and our "cheese" is constantly being moved. But Johnson says we have a choice in how we respond, and that choice affects much of our life. I agree. Change is a natural part of our entire life. Our bodies are constantly changing. If you think about it, over time, our passions and interests change too.

Change can be very good, but it can also be very troublesome. I believe life changes are one reason many friendships end. For example, a friend may move geographically, and even though both parties hope to remain friends, a break in the relationship ensues. Many a person has experienced a friend going through a significant milestone, like marriage or having kids, and then the relationship simply drifts because now the friends have little in common. In both situations, one person changes while the other is unable or unwilling to change. A corresponding change is required in order to maintain that intimate relationship.

Just as the clothes we wear and the furnishings in our homes are not the same fashion as they were fifteen to twenty years ago, the styles and patterns of our individual chairs are different today as well. I was in a home recently where the homeowner was raving about a chair in his living room. He told me how he and his wife had purchased it some twenty years ago and

---

[27]   Spencer Johnson, *Who Moved My Cheese? An A-Mazing Way to Deal with Change in Your Work and in Your Life* (New York: Putnam Adult, 1998).

paid top dollar for it. The chair has hardly been used and is in almost the same condition it was when it was purchased. Don't get me wrong, the chair is nice. But there is no way he or I would buy the same chair today. The fabric went out of style at least fifteen years ago, and, frankly, this "once-perfect" chair is now out of place. The rest of his home is fantastic, but there is nothing in it that matches the style of this chair.

Think about yourself for a moment. I bet what interests and excites you today is somewhat different from what fired you up ten years ago. It certainly is for me. The unfortunate thing is that all too often, we learn what another person's chairs are and think we can buy that same chair forever. We fail to understand that the many things we've learned in the past influence our passions and the things that excite us today as life evolves. Because we keep living and experiencing new things, our chairs, which were perfect twenty years ago, now may be completely out of style.

When we understand that the people we care about and desire to be intimate with will change, we can properly plan for, expect, and even get excited about this change. Change can be fun! And we can and should get excited about it.

It's worth noting that what we are excited and passionate about is rarely good or bad. Our chairs, no matter how they change, are simply an important part of who we are. These new chairs become part of our story like anything else. Understanding this and seeking to grow and learn together in relationship brings an even deeper closeness to the intimacy two people can share.

I've recently experienced this in my relationship with my son, Aaron. He and I have always had a pretty tight relationship. I was very active in Aaron's life through elementary, middle, and high school. But when Aaron entered his senior year of high school, his passions and interests started significantly changing. To be fair, they probably had been changing for years, but I hadn't noticed. I wasn't ready for it and didn't want the change to occur.

Aaron and I shared a love for wrestling. Aaron is good at the sport, and I enjoyed coaching him as he grew up as well as watching him compete at the high school level. We experienced great times together, talking about his matches and celebrating the victories. Frankly, we were both sharing an enjoyment of the same chairs. For years, I had hoped and dreamed that Aaron would compete in college. I looked forward to staying engaged with him as he progressed to the next level of competition. That was my plan, but it was not Aaron's. I had to learn to deal with this if I hoped to stay in an intimate relationship with my son.

Fortunately, I decided I wanted to maintain our connection and support my son. I wanted to engage with him where he was. This required me to commit to trying my hardest to learn continually what Aaron was passionate about in the here and now. In his first week of college, Aaron began taking pictures, really magnificent pictures. He discovered he honestly enjoyed being outdoors and taking pictures that captured the beauty of creation. He also realized he had a knack for it and that others benefited from his creativity with the camera. All he had to do was post one picture on Facebook and his grandma, along with half a dozen others, commented on it. I've never been into photography, but I have enjoyed learning about what my son is excited about. I've enjoyed seeing the world through his eyes and talking with him about the things he's experienced. Sometimes, when I see a beautiful sunset or another aspect of creation, I think, *Wow, I bet Aaron would have loved to photograph this.*

See, in Aaron's freshman year of high school, his chairs were of a style and pattern totally different from the ones that mattered to him during his freshman year of college. And they're different again today as he's grown older. Now, he's hardly ever out taking pictures. He's actively involved in all things golf. Five years from now, his chairs probably will have changed again. My job is to pay attention to the details and learn to appreciate whatever styles and patterns are in fashion for him. All the while, I need to remember that those styles and patterns will change, and there is nothing I can do to stop or change that. Rather, I can simply get excited about the change and embrace the journey of exploring and learning. So can you.

Truth Four: You Might Begin to Really Like Another's Chairs

I mentioned how much Aaron was into wrestling for many years and that we shared a love of the sport. But actually, I didn't always love wrestling. In fact, when Aaron started wrestling in kindergarten, I knew next to nothing about the sport. We had moved to a small town in Michigan where, unbeknownst to us, wrestling was king. The town's high school had won something like nine out of the past ten state wrestling championships. When Aaron came home from kindergarten with a note in his backpack about wrestling sign-ups and said he wanted to do it, I didn't know what we were getting ourselves into. I only knew my son was excited about it and I wanted to support him.

As I got involved and learned about the sport, it enabled us to share in different ways. I'll forever appreciate the youth club that highly encouraged parental involvement. I also started attending any coaching clinic I could find, and the best coaches helped me learn. I started wrestling myself with the bigger middle school and high school wrestlers. I found that I truly enjoyed it. Who knew that following my son's interest would turn into something I really enjoyed as well?

Now, twenty years later, wrestling is still a part of my life. I coached for roughly fifteen years. As a top coach, I won many awards. I've made a difference in many young wrestlers' lives. Wrestling, and specifically sharing life and Christian lessons with other coaches and with wrestlers I have coached, became a part of my pastoral ministry. Today, even though I'm no longer actively coaching, the sport of wrestling is still one of my chairs. Will it always be? I don't know.

I'm changing, just like Aaron. But unlike where I was fifteen years ago, I'm excited about the change!

My point in bringing all this up is to say that from time to time, when you really invest in buying another's chairs, you might begin to genuinely like those chairs. You might find enormous joy in the process of making those chairs your own. Buying another's chairs can open up new talents and abilities that were never obvious before. It can stretch us to become something different from who we are right now, something that is almost always for the better.

As one final illustration of this topic, consider your eating habits. Do you like the same things today that you did fifteen, twenty, or even forty years ago? My bet is that your culinary preferences have changed. In fact, it's likely that some of your favorite foods today are things you wouldn't have wanted anything to do with a few years or even months ago. What if you had never tried them? Buying another's chairs is much like sampling a new type of food—possibly a type of food you wouldn't have ever considered eating. Every once in a while, if you're open to it, you find a new meal so delicious it might even become your new favorite. Why not try something new? Why not buy another's chairs?

NEXT STEP

Your next step for this chapter is to choose to really know others you care about. Pick one person you are close to and consider how much you know about what they are presently excited about or deeply interested in. Do you know why? Test yourself. Write down what you believe their answer(s) would be. Then ask them. Tell them you care and are curious about the things that excite them. An amazing conversation might follow, one that almost certainly will help grow your intimacy.

CHAPTER 11

Commitment and Calling

My initial outline for this book did not include this chapter. It is also the chapter I spent the most time thinking about, and the one I most resisted writing. In fact, this chapter will probably be the one that most readers will either reject outright or, at a minimum, find fault with. Despite all that, it may be one of the most important chapters, if not *the* most important one, in the book. This chapter ultimately deals with what it takes for you to successfully have intimacy as the defining trait of your relationships. It is also where I outline what I believe to be the clearest, most intimate relationship I have ever experienced. I wholeheartedly believe that without both commitment and calling, we will never experience the intimacy that God desires for us.

Throughout this book, I've attempted to provide logical insights that would apply in every relationship situation regardless of race, religion, creed, sexual orientation, or any other life trait. Obviously, I'm a Christian, and I wrote this book from a Christian worldview. No book on intimacy from a Christian perspective would be sufficient without clearly discussing the most intimate relationship any of us can have—an intimate love relationship with the Lord. This is the most meaningful intimate relationship I have ever experienced. It is in a personal relationship with God where I truly discovered intimacy, and all the principles in this book apply equally to that relationship.

It is also in this relationship where the ideas in this chapter on commitment and calling are most clear. Some of you who are simply looking for the x's and o's of intimacy may be tempted to skip this chapter. It doesn't fit neatly into the formulaic "do this and don't do that" approach to building intimate relationships. But while you could skip ahead, I encourage you to read on with an open mind. Seek to learn whatever truth you can from my understanding of a relationship with God as it pertains to intimacy. Certainly, pay attention to the principles that apply to commitment and calling.

While closely related, commitment and calling are two different things. Often, you won't have one without the other. In my mind, they're interdependent. At a minimum, commitment—real, life-altering commitment—usually requires a calling. Otherwise, a person is not going to make the necessary commitment. In the case of intimacy, both commitment and calling are born out of a supernatural experience of intimacy.

In case you consider rejecting outright what I have just said, please think about why some who have learned about intimacy choose not to live in intimacy. What about those who read this book or attend one of my seminars but ultimately change little to nothing in their lives? Why don't these people experience intimacy? I propose that the answer has to do primarily with both commitment and calling. In many if not all cases, individuals who do not commit to intimacy have never experienced a real, intimate love relationship. The perfect example of such an intimate love relationship is found in the relationship available to us with Christ. Therefore, many people are unwilling to do what is necessary to have one.

Once someone experiences a real intimate love relationship, they will never be happy in relationships that are not that way. An intimate love relationship changes a person. It's as if our taste buds become awakened and we won't ever again settle for blandness. Once we've had the best, anything but the best is lacking. So, we live life realizing that the best is possible and desiring that in every relationship. And then we do what it takes: sacrifice, be hurt from time to time, take risks, be vulnerable, and give of ourselves to others so that intimacy will be the marker in more of our relations. But what if we have never experienced such a relationship in the first place? How do we begin? How does change occur? I believe we must be called to do so.

One thing I think most non-Christians like least about Christianity is the idea that people are "called" by God. But discussing this point is unavoidable if we are going to take the clear meaning and teaching of Scripture seriously. Many in the Christian church argue and debate vigorously over how God calls, who God calls, and the effects of God's calling. I have no intention of getting into any such debate here. As it relates to intimacy, I hope you and I can agree on three points. First, God calls us. Second, His calling is to enter an intimate love relationship with Him. And third, to have that relationship, we need to accept His calling.

Mark 10:17-27 illustrates better than most other passages of Scripture both the calling of the Lord and the commitment required to accept that calling. While this passage specifically relates to our eternal, spiritual relationship with God, I find close parallels with intimacy in our human relationships. In this account, a man approaches Jesus, asking what is necessary to "inherit eternal life" (v. 17). It sounds to me like he really is interested, much like you are interested in intimacy or you wouldn't be reading this book. Let's read this story from the Gospel of Mark:

> And as he was setting out on his journey, a man ran up and knelt before him and asked him, "Good Teacher,

what must I do to inherit eternal life?" And Jesus said to him, "Why do you call me good? No one is good except God alone. You know the commandments: 'Do not murder, Do not commit adultery, Do not steal, Do not bear false witness, Do not defraud, Honor your father and mother.'" And he said to him, "Teacher, all these I have kept from my youth." And Jesus, looking at him, loved him, and said to him, "You lack one thing: go, sell all that you have and give to the poor, and you will have treasure in heaven; and come, follow me." Disheartened by the saying, he went away sorrowful, for he had great possessions.

And Jesus looked around and said to his disciples, "How difficult it will be for those who have wealth to enter the kingdom of God!" And the disciples were amazed at his words. But Jesus said to them again, "Children, how difficult it is to enter the kingdom of God! It is easier for a camel to go through the eye of a needle than for a rich person to enter the kingdom of God." And they were exceedingly astonished, and said to him, "Then who can be saved?" Jesus looked at them and said, "With man it is impossible, but not with God. For all things are possible with God."

While there is a lot to digest from this passage, I want to focus on two central truths that apply not only to our prospect of an eternal relationship with our Savior but also to the process of building intimate relationships with others on earth. The first of these truths is that there is a genuine need for commitment. This is most evident in Jesus asking this man to sell everything and follow Him. Other than dying, Jesus basically asked for an ultimate commitment from this man. Sell everything! Burn the ships! Follow me! Jesus demanded a genuine commitment that was all in. And the second truth is that there is a need to respond to a calling. This is clearly seen in the answer Jesus gave to His disciples, explaining that the only way they could do what was necessary was through God's help, responding to His call.

As we drill down into this exchange to explore the essence of these two truths, I think it's important to look at not only what Jesus said but what both the rich man and Jesus asked. First, this man who approached Jesus seems to be clearly asking how he might "inherit eternal life." I see nothing in his question that shows he had any other interest but eternal life when talking to our Savior. While others in Jesus's time asked questions to trap Him, I don't see that in this exchange. Honestly, this man seems like a lot of men I assist in addiction recovery work. They want out of their addiction. These guys are serious. They come saying essentially the same thing: "teach me" or "show me" how to win this battle.

Jesus basically responded that this man needed only to follow the Ten Commandments. But it's important to note something the disciples noted: This command from Jesus is impossible for everyone. We all fail. None of us are perfect, and none of us will ever be able to follow all the laws perfectly. Jesus knows everything, and clearly Jesus knew this when He responded to this man's question. Though obviously I'm not Jesus and I can't know exactly what Jesus was thinking, I believe this was really a test to see how the rich man would respond. Better stated, I believe Jesus invited the man to express more clearly what was in his heart. While

Jesus, being fully God, already knew what was in this man's heart, He gave the man the opportunity to be vulnerable with Him. It was an opening for intimacy. Would the man fall on his face and say, "Teacher, I'm lost. There's no way I can do that. I'm a failure"? No, sadly, that wasn't his reply at all, though it should have been. Instead, his answer was similar to how we also might respond in the spotlight. Remember, this was a public exchange. Everyone was looking at this person who, on the surface, seemed to have it all together and seemed to ask the exact right question. Look at his reply, which was basically, "Yes, I've got all that. I've done all that since I was a boy."

Verse 21 is highly important: "Jesus . . . loved him." Despite this man's hiding the truth of his inability to live up to the holy standard that God demands, Jesus still wanted to engage with him. One thing I like about Jesus is that He says what we need to hear, regardless of what others might think. His next utterance cuts to the core of the matter of this man and what he really wanted. Jesus asked, in essence, "Will you commit?" The question the Lord asked this man is the same question He asks you and me: "Will you give up everything for a relationship with Me?" For this rich man, and unfortunately for most people, the answer to this question was and is no.

It's not hard to see why so many of us balk at this challenge and end up walking away dejected. Complete commitment to any worthwhile endeavor is difficult and rare. Yet Jesus leaves no doubt that in order to be in an intimate relationship with Him (which in other Scripture He defined as having "eternal life" or entering heaven), we must fully commit. At the same time, through this encounter, He brings home the point that it is almost impossible for those who are "rich" to do this. As I see it, our reluctance to part with our wealth, of one kind or another, inhibits our ability to form intimate relationships not only with our Savior but with our counterparts on earth.

I believe that in America we often don't realize exactly how "rich" we all are. I'm not specifically thinking of financial wealth, although that argument could be made as well. I'm talking about all our other wealth. I'm talking about relational wealth, positional wealth, and status wealth. All too often, we are rich and unwilling to part with our wealth if intimacy requires us to do so. For example, if there are unknown character defects, habits, or addictions that are part of the real you, what would happen if you shared the full truth about yourself with others? How would this affect your wealth? How might it affect your spouse, partner, friends, workforce, church, or neighborhood? If your spouse learned about the real you, it might cost you your marriage. Becoming known might cost you your job, your standing in the community, or your position in the church. You might have to pay the price of facing head-on the façade you've sold others about yourself.

Most of us are rich in one way or another, and for many of us, any command to depart from that wealth is too much to bear. We can't sign up to be that committed and would rather simply keep what we have. For this very reason, we remain in relationships devoid of real intimacy. And it's for this reason many will not follow Christ as well—much like the rich man in this encounter.

I'll never forget the day I approached my best male friend and told him I had never let him know the real me. This dear brother had served with me in church for many years. We were close. We were fishing buddies. We went on trips together, led Bible studies together, and had private prayer time with each other. But he didn't know my darkest secrets. He truly didn't know me. When I approached him with the plan of finally allowing him to know the real me, I didn't know what to expect. I needed to apologize for being false around him and not trusting him to know me. While I wanted and hoped for forgiveness and growth in our relationship, I knew that instead I might experience rejection, separation, and possibly an end to our friendship. I'm grateful he didn't let that happen. He certainly could have. For me, pursuing intimacy with others meant a commitment to intimacy, and that commitment could have cost me a cherished friendship. This friendship was a big part of my wealth.

There is a distressing reality that all types of people resist making the commitments essential to intimacy. I see this all the time in addiction recovery groups. Men will come in wanting (really wanting) to be healed of addiction. They are informed and taught how to fully surrender. Leaders and group facilitators model and share with these individuals how to live and function in sobriety through a recovery program. There are things they need to do as part of this program to experience sobriety in their own lives, such as sharing a complete and honest confession. These actions might cost them virtually everything they know, including their material wealth. Unfortunately, that commitment is too much for a lot of them, so they remain stuck in their addiction—just like the rich man in his encounter with Jesus. This truly is heartbreaking, much like it must have been for Jesus that day.

Here's my question for you related to this point: How committed are you to intimacy? Unless you are fully invested, willing to put it above everything, you will likely not find intimacy no matter how hard you search for it. At least, you won't find complete, life-altering intimacy that is readily available on this earth.

Commitment, though, is not the only thing on Jesus's mind in this passage. I sense from looking at the questions He asked his disciples that they were rocked to the core by Jesus's words to this man. You also might be shocked right now. Their question in Matthew 10:26 was the right question: "Then who can be saved?" I think they truly got it. I think their question shows the intimate relationship they were already in with Jesus. They didn't carry on as if they understood. They knew they couldn't fulfill what Jesus had asked on their own. His disciples did not hide, act proud, or remind Jesus that they in fact had been willing to sell everything and follow Him. Their dismay was a true feeling for them, even though most of His disciples had done just that. Most had given up everything they had and knew to follow Jesus. And yet there was genuine humility and vulnerability in their question. Likely, this was the same vulnerability Jesus wished the rich man had been willing to show.

To sum this up, the disciples were saying, "Teacher, we can't do this. We can't keep the law. We fail in our commitment. What does this mean for us? Are we forever lost?" This is honesty at its core. Not only were these men being transparent about their feelings and doubts, they were also sharing their doubt about what they were doing in relationship with Jesus at all.

The disciples' open and honest question led Jesus to the second essential truth I mentioned earlier: No one can be in a relationship with Him (have eternal life) apart from God doing the work. In Christian circles, we refer to this as "being called." The biblical writers used different methods and language to convey the same idea. You will see "called," "chosen," "drawn," and "predestined." All convey the same idea: God does the calling and the work in salvation, and in order for us to experience eternal life, it fully depends on His calling and His work. Consider the following passages, which further show this truth:

- John 6:44: "No one can come to me unless the Father who sent me draws him. And I will raise him up on the last day."

- 1 Corinthians 1:26–29: "For consider your calling, brothers: not many of you were wise according to worldly standards, not many were powerful, not many were of noble birth. But God chose what is foolish in the world to shame the wise; God chose what is weak in the world to shame the strong;

God chose what is low and despised in the world, even things that are not, to bring to nothing things that are, so that no human being might boast in the presence of God."

- Romans 8:30: "And those whom he predestined he also called, and those whom he called he also justified, and those whom he justified he also glorified."

- John 15:16: "You did not choose me, but I chose you and appointed you that you should go and bear fruit and that your fruit should abide, so that whatever you ask the Father in my name, he may give it to you."

- Deuteronomy 7:6: "For you are a people holy to the LORD your God. The LORD your God has chosen you to be a people for his treasured possession, out of all the peoples who are on the face of the earth."

In all these verses—some in Jesus's own words, some in the words of the apostle Paul, and one from the Old Testament—the Scriptures affirm that the only way we can be fully committed and in an intimate relationship with Him is if we are first called by Him and if we then answer that call.

In my view, intimacy between people requires the same thing. I fully believe that for any human being to experience the fullness of intimacy, that person needs to feel a call to intimacy. And they need to respond to that call by becoming fully committed.

This commitment will lead them to do the things I've outlined in this book. It will change their life to a point where being honest, transparent, open, loving, caring, and selfless becomes the norm. It is my personal prayer that God might use this book to extend such a call to you.

For me, my pastor's sermon series on forgiveness was both God's invitation and God's calling for me to pursue intimacy. Ultimately, it was about my need for forgiveness. But more importantly, it was a call to trust Him and commit to doing what was necessary to receive that forgiveness. I knew the commitment He was calling me to. While I didn't know everything that would be required, I knew the starting point. I also knew that all of what I believed to be my wealth was on the line and would be, in a sense, put on the altar before God. I became willing to be known and to trust God, even if it cost me my marriage, my family, my career, and my friends. What I found was the same thing many others have found when they made the same commitments to God: He never fails.

Please note, before I surrendered to that call and commitment, the Lord had already richly blessed me, regardless of whether I fully recognized it. Many of the people who walked with Jesus in His day, and even the bystanders during His earthly ministry, experienced blessing simply by being around Jesus. Many experienced some of Jesus. Yet only a select few experienced all of a relationship with Jesus. Those who did and those who do today are in an intimate relationship with Him. In the same way, after responding to the Lord's calling years ago, I went from receiving partial blessings to the fullness of what God wanted for me all along.

Those who have not responded to a calling and made a commitment to intimacy may experience only touches of intimacy. They may receive common grace and experience the partial benefits that we all receive from relationships—even those that are not completely intimate. But those who respond to a call foremost to an intimate relationship with the Lord Jesus Christ and then to a call to live their lives seeking intimacy in human relationships will experience something much richer, much fuller, and much more rewarding. Again, I hope that is you.

NEXT STEP

Your next step for this chapter is to thank God for His calling and His work in your life if you have an intimate relationship with Him. If you don't yet have that, your next step is to make the decision to surrender everything from the richness of your life to begin an intimate relationship with Him and others.

CHAPTER 12

Walking in Intimacy

When I first began hosting "What Is Intimacy?" seminars for men, I had not planned on including a time slot for a discussion of what it looks like practically to walk in intimacy. That was a foolish omission on my part. I'm not sure exactly why I didn't plan on speaking on this subject other than thinking I would just teach about what intimacy is, what it is not, and what it will take to make our relationships more intimate. All of that changed when I set aside a few minutes at the end of the seminar for questions and answers and volunteered to stay afterward to discuss topics of interest. It turned out that I was at the venue for roughly another hour with almost all the seminar attendees still there asking questions. They had already been with me for more than six hours! Most of the questions centered on my personal experience of living in the here and now with the knowledge I've attained. Many of the men that day wanted to know what to expect if they radically changed their lives to become men of intimacy.

I hope this chapter provides something similar for you. My goal is to answer what I think might be some lingering questions. I want to share some practical details of what it means to walk in intimacy. This includes suggestions for things you might do in your own life. While I'll give you some specifics in this chapter, I'd like to again remind you to become an "Intimacy Fan" by joining the subscriber list at **www.RedefiningIntimacy.org**. By being on this list (which is totally free), you'll get a biweekly email from me with additional practical tips to further grow in intimacy.

In addition to laying out practical life tips, I also seek in this chapter to paint for you an appropriate before-and-after picture of my life. Throughout the book, I've shared parts of my past, so you probably already have a pretty good idea of the before picture. I've also already shared a couple of stories about how I've applied the principles in this book, so you may have already drawn most of my after picture. My before-intimacy and after-intimacy pictures are so starkly different that, in some ways, it's hard to recognize it's really me in both of them.

Finally, one last goal in this chapter is to introduce my wife, Tammy, and allow you to hear directly from her. I hope her perspective as both a woman and the person who knows me best will be meaningful to you.

With regard to my first goal, I'm guessing you might like some specific recommendations for actions you can take to move toward more intimate relationships in your own life. I'll be glad to offer a few in just a moment. But before doing so, I'd like to make two strong recommendations. First, and this won't surprise you because you've heard me refer to this many times already, consider seeking professional help for yourself as a person. This is especially true if you struggle with an addiction, have experienced significant past trauma, or are depressed. We all need help sometimes, and trained therapists exist for a reason.

Second, get involved with others in group settings where you can grow in intimacy alongside others. As mentioned earlier, small groups have been essential to my growth. The life group I attend weekly with my wife has been incredibly meaningful to both me and Tammy. We've seen firsthand how we can be real about our past and current struggles and receive understanding, compassion, support, and encouragement. Especially in the early stages of recovery, being involved with other men who were struggling in the same way as I was proved critical to my success. I can't imagine being well today apart from having been really known in a group setting.

I do want to provide a word of caution, though, pertaining to groups. Much like what I discussed earlier about safe people, some groups are not safe, even though they should be. Groups not designed with intimacy at their base are probably not safe. Over the years, I have been involved in numerous religious groups in which members of the group weren't really known. These groups weren't intimate at all. They should have been. But often members would not deeply discuss their own struggles or problems. Almost certainly they would not discuss the root causes of their struggles. Why? The answer may be that most people wrongly believe that if the truth about their personal struggles, problems, and character defects became known, the other members would not welcome them in their typical church small group. What's tragically sad about this reality is that church small groups should be an ideal place for intimacy to occur.

With all of that communicated, how might you apply this information I've given you regarding intimacy? What are practical things you can do? I'm glad you asked.

Application of Important Truths and Principles Learned along the Way

1. Control what you can control.

This truth might be one of the greatest principles I have learned. It applies to virtually everything in life. I've already discussed control a great deal in chapter seven, so I won't repeat myself here. But I would like to focus on two related questions. The first is, what are the things that are in my control or that I can potentially control? The second is, what things are outside my control? I've discovered that I must, as quickly as possible, recognize the difference if I'm going to be the best I can be. The list that follows is not all-inclusive, and it reiterates a few points I've previously discussed; I'm only repeating them here to build on the practical ways we can apply the principles.

What things are in my control? What can I control?

- **I can choose how I invest my time and whom I will be close to.** We don't choose the family we are born into. And most of us don't get to choose our boss, coworkers, neighbors, or many other people we share life with. However, we can choose to spend more quality time with people who are willing to and desire to be in intimate relationships with us. The converse is also true. We can choose to distance ourselves from and limit our time with those people who are not interested in being in an intimate relationship with us.

I have a very close family member about whom I ultimately had to say to myself, "This person really doesn't significantly care about me. This person isn't interested in seeking to know me, my interests, or my passions. No matter what I give to the relationship, I will see no similar return. I need to let this relationship be what it is and focus my attention and time where it is meaningful." This was hard to do. I have family members who don't understand it; family members who think I'm wrong. Here's the thing: all of us have a very limited amount of time and emotional capacity. In my own case, I prefer to invest the time I have into relationships with people who I know care about me. These same people choose to invest their own time and emotional capacity into really knowing me. You have the right to decide for yourself whom you will invest your time and heart into. This is where you can wield control.

- **I can choose to feel and empathize with others.** I've heard from others (mostly men) that they have a hard time feeling and empathizing with other people. The fact that something is hard has nothing to do with whether it is possible. We can train ourselves, and we can grow. I've often found that the best things in life are hard to get and require effort. Sharing feelings and empathizing with others is simply a choice. There are tools that can help, including feeling charts and other books that train us to use our feelings. I recognized I simply needed to make the choice to stop and focus my attention to feel and empathize. As I've practiced this in real life, it has gotten easier.

- **I can be known.** Let me share something that might initially make you think I'm going against this point: Many people don't care about you, and many probably don't want to know you. So what? Many people are hurting, miserable, selfish human beings. Yet there are people who *do* want to know you. We may never come to understand how our being known might affect others. Yes, being willing to be known puts us in a vulnerable position. And yes, being willing to be known may lead to some hurt and rejection. But being known is an amazing thing. It leads to freedom. It leads to love. Being known leads to genuine, intimate relationships with others. It enhances and feeds our positive self-esteem when we realize we have friends who know us and still love us. Clearly, there are people in whom it's not safe for us to confide everything about us or our past. We have every right and responsibility to be careful with what we share and how quickly we share it. However, it is in our control to be a person who seeks whenever possible to be known.

- **I can admit to my mistakes and failures.** Over the past nine years of living in intimacy, being willing to admit to my mistakes and failures has been a positive character attribute in which I have significantly grown. For most of my life, I tried to hide my mistakes and failures. I sought to blame others for them. I almost always had an excuse. You want to know what I've found? The vast majority of people are very understanding. Most people are remarkably willing to forgive our mistakes and failures because most people realize they need the same forgiveness for their own mistakes. There is something especially refreshing today in hearing someone say, "You know what? I'm really sorry. That mistake was solely on me. Please forgive me." It's so refreshing because it is so very rare. A great many people live in fear of owning their shortcomings—shortcomings we all have. When you make mistakes, you can control what you do about them.

- **I can control whether I will be accountable to others.** Our desire for independence and freedom in America is a great thing in certain ways. But in terms of accountability, it can be a tremendous weakness. Most of us rebel strongly against the idea of being accountable to someone else, especially if we don't have to be. As I've worked to build intimacy with others, I've found that it is a powerful benefit to hold myself accountable to others. It's helpful to me to know I will need to share with those close to me when I fail. While you may not be like me, I'm much more likely to avoid detrimental behavior if I will be embarrassed about it being known. This isn't my only reason for doing what's right, but I'm happy to have this as another motivator. It's also exciting to know I will have the privilege of sharing my successes with others who will celebrate with me. We can control whether we seek true friends to whom we will be accountable.

What things are outside my control?

- **I cannot control who will choose to be intimate with me.** The hardest thing for me to accept even now, and the thing that hurts the worst, is that some people will choose not to pursue an intimate relationship with me. We cannot control whether another person pursues intimacy with us, and that's something that can be difficult to live with. Please understand, I did not say you can't have a powerful influence. The way we live our lives can indeed encourage others to want to have an intimate relationship with us. But we cannot control this. We must accept that despite our best efforts, another person may simply choose not to be intimate with us.

- **I cannot control whether another person will accept my help or get the help they desperately need.** One of the saddest things in life is when we would like to help someone and they choose to reject our help. Some people are simply too proud to receive the help they need. In these situations, we have zero control and must understand that the giving and receiving of help is a two-way experience. The same thing applies when we ultimately aren't the right person to help. Before my mother passed away,

I always hoped that one day she would get the psychological help she severely needed. I hoped she would realize that her unwillingness to avail herself of that help had seriously hurt other people, and still was hurting them. Sadly, no matter how much I hoped, I could not control whether my mom sought the psychological treatment she needed. No one could control this except her. I could cite many other examples, but let me share one specific way this happens in marriage. There are many women urging their husbands to get the help they need to free themselves from the use of pornography. If these husbands do not decide to make sexual holiness happen for themselves, there will be no change. These wives cannot control their husbands. This is a tough reality to swallow, but it is true.

- **I cannot control how another person feels.** This point was covered in chapter seven, so I will only reemphasize that most people regularly battle with this truth. We really do try to control how other people are going to feel. Don't resist allowing yourself to be known or sharing your own feelings out of fear of how others' feelings will be affected. Be willing to engage in truthful discussions, even arguments at times, if it will help resolve differences and allow growth in relationships.

- **I cannot control what tomorrow brings.** This seems like it should go without saying, but I believe many people live and act as if the opposite were true. While there is nothing wrong with planning, none of us really knows what tomorrow will bring. We don't even know if there is a tomorrow for us. Often, our attempts to control the future only result in worry, anxiety, and disappointment. I wonder what would happen in our relationships alone if we believed we didn't have a tomorrow? What if we treated our friends and family as if today was all we had? See, the flip side of this "what you can't control" (i.e., tomorrow) is what you can control. You can control only what you do right now, and that is this moment, today.

2. Be grateful.

If there is any one thing people can do that has the potential to make a significant difference in every area of life, it is to be grateful. Living with an "attitude of gratitude" really makes an enormous difference. Every human being truly has so much to be grateful for. At a minimum, we are alive, and we're created in the image of God (Gen. 1:27). When we choose to be grateful, it focuses our attention on the positive. We remind ourselves that things could certainly be worse. More than that, though, gratitude helps us correctly see that we are doing so much better than many others.

Specifically, as it pertains to our relationships becoming more intimate, being grateful for the friends and family we have also makes a big difference. It is common for people to compare. It's easy to look at others and say, "They have it better." We are, by nature, an envious people, so much so that two of the Ten Commandments warn against it. Gratitude settles us into reality. If I have one friend who knows me, I mean really knows me, and still wants to be my friend, I have more than many people do today who are not known. If that relationship with that one friend is growing and becoming more intimate over time, I have something to be cherished. I can and should be extremely grateful.

Being grateful is good, but expressing gratitude is better. When we are grateful, it's natural to want to express it. Let me ask you a question. When was the last time you told a close friend you were grateful that he or she is your friend? Have you shared with someone close to you recently that you are so grateful you get to share this life with them? When was the last time someone told you that? Okay, that question might have hurt, because you may not remember the last time it happened. But if you do remember, you likely recall exactly how it made you feel. It made you feel important, valued, appreciated, loved, and cared for. We need more of that. Living life as a grateful person gives you the opportunity to make a tremendous impact in the lives of others, including total strangers, by nurturing them and introducing positivity into their day. Imagine how much more you could affect those you know really well. What could living out being grateful mean to your relationships?

3. **Be present; don't push.**

Speaking of gratitude, I am extremely grateful I have a "point man" in my life. Some might use the word *mentor* for this friend of mine. Others in the addiction recovery world might use the word *sponsor*. The friend I'm thinking about has been there for me in the past, and he's with me today to "point" me to the truth. He knows me, cares about me, and has the freedom to tell me what I need to hear, whether or not I want to hear it. One thing he has reminded me of several times recently is to "be present, but don't push." This reminder has most often come when I want to pressure (another word for control) another person to do something different, to be better, or to quit doing things that are not good for him or her. My motive in pressuring others is well-intended. The problem is that my pushing is not helpful, despite what I might think. This is especially true with regard to my children. The reality often is that our pushing pushes people away.

But my friend doesn't just say, "don't push." He says, *"be present,* don't push." That's an important distinction. Being present is essential in intimate relationships. Being present means I am fully there. My mind and heart are in the relationship. I'm not distracted or distant. I'm not pouting. My focus is not on exerting my will, regardless of my intentions. I'm simply "there" in the relationship. This allows me to be a true help. It enables me to be a needed friend.

I think many of us don't realize the impact we have by simply "being there" with someone who knows we really love them and care about them. When we are in intimate relationships, presence is an enormous deal. I love my wife. I love spending time with her. Being in her presence is life-giving. I can say the same about my relationship with the Lord.

Our simple presence enables a person to see that we are worthy of being listened to. This results in closeness. I've found I'm much more effective at influencing my friends by really caring about them and being present in their lives. Being present allows us to model behavior. Being present allows others to ask us for direction they are willing to accept. It's rare to experience others in the world being fully present with us. Being present is often the opposite of what most everyone experiences in relationships. When we experience someone being present with us, we naturally want to hear what they have to say. Commit right now to be more present in your relationships and to "stop pushing." You'll likely find you don't have to push and will have more influence than you have had in the past.

4. We are all suffering or struggling with something.

It's natural to think our experiences are unique to us. It's also easy to believe "There is no one like me. No one can understand what I am feeling and experiencing right now." In reality, we have far more in common with each other than we might like to imagine. In fact, as our knowledge about science and biology has expanded, it has become known that "all human beings are 99.9 percent identical in their genetic makeup."[28] It's pretty incredible to me to think that another man or woman who might have a totally different skin color than me, or be much taller or shorter than me, or have many other physical differences from me, is only less than one-tenth of 1 percent genetically different from me. Similarly, most of my life experiences have been or are currently being experienced by others.

This reality should affect the way we think in at least two ways. First, it should cause us to see ourselves as similar to others. For example, many of us struggle with being

---

[28] "Genetics vs. Genomics Fact Sheet," National Human Genome Research Institute, accessed June 14, 2024, https://www.genome.gov/about-genomics/fact-sheets/Genetics-vs-Genomics.

overly self-critical. We feel like we're the only one who makes this mistake or that mistake. In these instances, we beat ourselves up for things we would never beat up somebody else for. When we properly understand our commonality with others, we gain a more proper and healthy view of self.

From my work in addiction recovery circles, a strong feeling of aloneness is one area in which addicts struggle the most. Addicts frequently believe they are alone in their struggle, although many other people suffer in the same way and have overcome. One of the things that must happen for addicts to develop long-term sobriety is that they must see themselves not as alone but as connected to others who understand them and can relate. Understanding and believing that everyone is struggling with something moves us to a closer connection with others and away from feelings of loneliness.

Second, being aware that we are all suffering or struggling with something should cause us to be more cognizant of the actual needs of others around us. Every day, we encounter a great number of hurting people. These people may not only feel totally alone but may also be totally alone. A proper understanding of the commonality of suffering enables us to be a help to others. In relationships, keeping a perspective that others are not perfect, are struggling with the same sin condition, and are in need of grace and compassion is essential to our growing in intimacy.

It's for this reason that, over time, I've become increasingly willing to share at least part of my story with those I interact with. I don't get into the details of my story with everyone, but I do help others understand that I'm someone who is trustworthy and will support them in becoming better than they are today. Since I began grounding myself to living in intimacy, a number of people have sought my help in overcoming similar problems in their own lives. I've yet to meet a person who is not struggling with something.

5. **Life is a journey. Every day is a new opportunity to improve.**

My primary accountability partner likes to use the term *journey* to discuss the path we are on in life. I think his idea is that when we go on a journey, we are going to experience a lot of different things, and possibly things we didn't plan for or expect. Things go right, but things also go wrong. Now, most of us have made directional mistakes when traveling that took us down the wrong road. On those occasions, we had to turn around and get back on track. Life and relationships are much the same. A relationship is really nothing more than a journey shared by two broken people who have made mistakes in the past, are still making mistakes daily, and will continue to make them in the future.

There will always be a need to improve ourselves, both in areas that are seen and in those that are unseen. For example, there have been several times when I've needed to make a course correction in my eating, as signaled by my pants not fitting the way they should. I can choose today in any area of life to focus my attention on getting better. In the case of my pants not fitting, I simply need to choose to eat better and exercise more. In regard to the unseen, I've more than once caught myself being negative and judgmental. I don't have to stay that way. I can decide to work on being positive, understanding, and empathetic.

But sometimes we focus too heavily on our failures at the expense of thinking about areas of improvement. We brood over our mistakes and missed opportunities, and fail to recognize improvements in our character, trustworthiness, and ability to share our feelings. When our character improves and our attitudes change for the better, these things make a difference in our life and the lives of others. When our pants fit better and our health improves because of our efforts to live healthier, we deserve to recognize that. We should pause and give ourselves and others a bit more grace for areas of weakness we all have. We should also celebrate our victories and growth more than we do.

I was in a church service recently where the pastor was preaching a message about the heart and the need for the heart to be renewed. This got me thinking about the fact that, as Christians, we are called to have a heart that is renewed day by day. The apostle Paul, in his second letter to the Corinthians, spoke about the many challenges he and those in the church were facing. His focus through it all was that "as grace extends to more and more people it may increase thanksgiving, to the glory of God" (2 Cor. 4:15). Immediately after making that statement, Paul shares this beautiful passage with us:

> So we do not lose heart. Though our outer self is wasting away, our inner self is being renewed day by day. For this light momentary affliction is preparing for us an eternal weight of glory beyond all comparison, as we look not to the things that are seen but to the things that are unseen. For the things that are seen are transient, but the things that are unseen are eternal. (2 Cor. 4:16–18)

I invite you not to lose heart. No matter what you or I may go through, we are on a journey. If we're in an intimate relationship with God, we know where our eternal home is. Spend some time thinking about and focusing on the things that are unseen. I understand that

Paul was primarily speaking about heaven and what is prepared for us there, but God is doing things in us and to our souls right now that are just as eternal. Consider what God has done already in your life. Consider what He is doing right now. Praise Him for the things He has yet to do in your life as you walk with Him and others in intimacy. Each day, really each moment, is a new opportunity for us to improve—to the glory of God!

Some Practical Day-to-Day Ideas

I hope each of the above principles will serve you well as you seek to have more intimate relationships. Now, I want to share some additional ideas you might wish to implement, along with practical examples. As you read, think about ways you can take these ideas and incorporate them into your life to bring about positive changes.

- **Be honest about character defects and work on them.** Pause with me for a moment and think about your best friend. What are his or her biggest character defects? Does he or she know yours? Until nine years ago, I *never* talked about my character defects. I hid them from everyone, including myself. This had at least two negative effects. First, it kept me living underneath a mountain of shame. Second, it kept me from improving. When I started being honest with myself and others, the shame began to go away.

I could finally allow myself to work on those defects. My close friends were a big part of my moving beyond them. Friends who knew my defects and were willing to share theirs with me helped make the journey much easier. Who in your life could you do that with? How might your life and theirs be different if you more frequently were open with each other about your character defects?

- **Optimize your date-night seating.** This point is a practical example of a simple thing we can do to foster the environment for intimacy to grow. It may seem silly, but something as effortless as choosing the right seat at a meal can be meaningful. Opting for the right seat relates directly to my point above about being present. Which seat do you choose when you're at a restaurant? Do you think about it? Visual stimuli easily distract most men. But actually, it's not just men. Women notice other people just the same. When I go out to eat with someone I care about, I want to be present with that person. I want to focus on them. I don't want to be distracted by anything, as far as I can help it. One way I make this easier is to sit where I will be the least distracted. For example, if we're out and there are big-screen TVs showing sporting events, I'm going to sit where my eyes have the least possibility of seeing a TV. I'm willing to ask a server to seat my wife and me at a different table if necessary. This example of date-night seating applies to many things if we simply exercise some common sense. We can choose to keep our phone in our pocket or purse, or not even bring it to meetings. We can choose to turn the music down or even off to better hear what someone is saying. There are many ways to show someone you care about them and what they have to communicate.

- **Be willing to try new things.** In chapter ten, I wrote about buying Tammy's chairs. As I shared there, when we engage in learning about what others care about, we often learn to enjoy those things as well. Our life experiences become much fuller when we do so. But that's not all. When I say, "Be willing to try new things," I'm not only talking about one person in the relationship trying something the other person enjoys. There is often something interesting that happens when two people in an intimate relationship try something new together. This is true even if they don't end up enjoying the new thing being tried. These opportunities give both individuals the opportunity to talk, feel, learn, and experience together. Questions arise and get answered, which allows the pair to grow even closer. "How does this impact you?" "What does this remind you of?" "How do you feel about this?" I could go on and on about the questions that can be asked and answered between them. We were made to experience life, and life is so much richer when experienced with others.

- **Be careful with sex.** There may have been no one thing more broken after the fall than sexual relations between a man and a woman. Even for those who haven't become addicted to sex or those who have steered clear of the use of pornography, our ideas related to sex and the way we "use" sex are dangerous. I wrote "use" because, honestly, I'm afraid that is what many people do. The wonderful benefits of sex can become nothing more than our drug of choice.

These days, I try to be very cautious about being sexual with my wife if I am experiencing feelings of hurt, pain, abandonment, or loneliness. What I want to avoid is using sex (even God-honoring sex with my wife) to deal with negative life emotions. Please don't mistake me; there is a healthy "sense of uplifting" that proper, regular marital sex has for both husband and wife. I believe God designed us that way. But we should be careful and periodically evaluate why we want sex. Is it simply because it is so enjoyable, and I want it? Is it because, in a marital context, God has given my wife to me and me to my wife? Or is it because I'm so connected and in love with my wife that this simply is a wonderfully natural way of expressing that love and connection, understanding that it will be great for both of us?

Further, and this might apply more to husbands than to anyone else, please be very careful with your motives. For most of my first twenty years of marriage, I hate to say that many of the nice things I did for my wife were done with the hope of having sex in mind. If we were going to have a date night or enjoy a romantic evening, just the two of us, I had an expectation of sex. In a sad way, what I was often communicating to my wife was that she was an object of my sexual expression. People don't like to talk that way or think that we act that way, but we sometimes can, and do. Here's a good question to ask: "If I knew sex was definitely not going to happen, would I still do things the same way?" If the answer is no, you can probably bet that sex, not intimacy, is more important to you. If we are consistently seeking to honor and love our spouse, to get to know our spouse better, to be more connected, and to empathize and feel with our spouse, sex becomes a natural by-product, and even if it doesn't, it's still wonderful that we get those other things.

One last point related to sex occurred to me that I'd like to share with you. My views of sex were distorted because of my upbringing. I've struggled with learning what is the healthy norm. I want to be certain I am always treating Tammy with the love and admiration she deserves. That said, I'm still a man, and I still get easily aroused by my beautiful wife. I'm interested in sex as much today as I was ten years ago. The difference is that I don't need sex. I need intimacy. I bring this up because there are a lot of sex-related things that people do, and it's important for us to balance those with what is healthy.

For example, a couple of years into recovery, I noticed there were many times when I simply enjoyed watching my wife get dressed. Is there anything inherently wrong with me watching my wife get dressed? Probably not. Still, I questioned within myself what my motivation was in doing so. I apologized to Tammy for many years of her simply being an object at these times. Since then, I've committed to being very careful when I look at her in certain situations. I choose to look at her with honor and not in some sick way to please myself. This might be an area where most people don't struggle at all. But I encourage every reader to be careful with sex and sexual stimuli.

- **Talk less, listen more.** This is a very simple statement, but doing it routinely is hard for many of us. One way people can tell whether we are present is in the way we listen. Often, while they're speaking, we are so busy planning how we're going to respond or exactly what we're going to say that we are not truly listening. I've sought to apply this idea of "talking less and listening more" by inserting more feeling into my listening. I've found that I have a hard time speaking and feeling at the same time. If I listen to someone else with the goal of hearing what they have to say, feeling with them as they say it, and processing what I'm hearing, I'm naturally going to talk less. From this comes an added benefit: the person I'm engaged in conversation with becomes more likely to really listen to me. Plus, I will, by my actions, have increased the likelihood that both of us will grow in intimacy.

- **Be more forgiving.** This bullet point serves as a reminder that we all need forgiveness. It is also a reminder that we tend as humans not to be forgiving because we are independent and selfish. We habitually fail to think about just how much we've been forgiven for and how much we need forgiveness daily as we live our lives. May I make a suggestion? When you think you are forgiving enough, seek to forgive more. Maintain an attitude such that throughout the day you will respond to the mistakes of others with forgiveness whenever you have an opportunity. Especially in relationships where you are seeking intimacy, it is vital that you operate from a base of forgiveness. Even our best friends make mistakes that can hurt us. If we approach our relationships with an attitude of forgiveness, I think we will recognize far less the minor imperfections in others and recognize far more the value in dear friends who love us and care about us despite their personal flaws.

- **Be someone others want to be intimate with.** Though I rightly stated that we cannot control whether someone else chooses to be intimate with us, we can have a significant influence. When we choose to pursue intimacy daily, seeking to live in relationships marked by intimacy, two important things happen naturally. First, we set an example for others to watch and follow; we all need examples and models to follow. Obviously, we have Jesus Christ as our perfect model and should look to imitate Him. But others who respect us and care about us look to us as an example. They may not be following Christ. They may not even know or care about Christ. They know you, assuming you are letting yourself be known. When intimacy is a defining characteristic of your life, others will see that, as you model living in intimate relationships. You might well be the reason someone else starts pursuing intimacy.

Second, we learn that we need to limit how many people we can truly be intimate with. We may want to be deeply intimate with everyone, but that's not realistic or possible. Each of us has limitations. For example, there is no person who gets more than twenty-four hours in a day. We are also limited in our emotional capacity. Think about a time when someone you cared deeply about shared something personal they were going through that you couldn't even imagine how you would respond to if you were in their situation. If you really empathized with them and felt some of what they were feeling, it was probably draining for you. It's natural to feel spent after something like that. How much emotional energy did you have immediately afterward? Very little, I suspect. Because of our limitations, we must be careful to choose who we are going to allow into our inner circle. While Jesus walked with His twelve and had thousands of people He influenced and affected in His earthly ministry, He kept only three closest to Him. Peter, James, and John were His inner circle and the men He was most intimate with. If Jesus, being both fully God and fully man, allowed Himself to have deep, intimate relationships with just three of the twelve disciples, shouldn't we, too, be selective in the people we fully invest in? In finding the right people to give your full self to, it helps to be a person worthy of someone else giving their full self as well. Strive to be a person whose thoughts, feelings, and actions are those that others would desire to welcome into their lives. Even if they don't, you will make a marked impact on the people around you.

A Before-and-After Picture

As I close this chapter and the book, I want to share one last time exactly how much intimacy has affected me. This time I thought it might be good for you to hear from my closest friend from her point of view. My wife, Tammy, has shared this journey with me as my life partner. She has had to forgive me many times and has seen me at my best and worst. I value her perspective more than anyone else's. I hope hearing from her will be a blessing for you.

To gain her insight, I sat down and interviewed Tammy. I gave her in advance a list of ten questions I thought might help you, the reader. What follows is from Tammy's heart. It's her personal experience as we have walked this journey. The questions I asked are in boldface. I did not hold back any of her answers. Sometimes I followed up on something Tammy shared with additional questions, as I wanted to better hear her heart and empathize with her. This exercise alone was of additional help to us. It allowed me to more deeply understand her experience, and it gave me a fresh chance to ask for forgiveness for ways I had hurt her in the past.

1. **Thinking back to the way I used to be before fully pursuing intimacy, what do you see as the biggest change in me as a person?**

    I answer this question more about us in our marriage relationship. I feel like you see me now. There were times in our first twenty years of marriage when I felt like you didn't know me, or care to really know me. You only pursued surface knowledge and basic day-to-day information from me or about me.

    Since entering recovery and allowing yourself to be known, you have desired to know me—my dreams, desires, and fears. I would also say that in the past, I couldn't count on you to do what you said you would do or be honest about things. That has been a big change. It's been a 180 there.

2. How have I changed relationally with you?

You don't hide physically or emotionally. In the past, upon getting home from work, you would go off in our bedroom and hide, it seemed. You would also not talk much about what was going on internally with you. Now, you don't run off when you come home. We have real conversations. There doesn't seem to be any more hiding. I no longer feel like I'm by myself in a lot of stuff.

3. How has the change to radically pursuing intimacy affected or changed our marriage?

This is a fairly short answer: I feel like we connect better relationally. I no longer feel responsible for your mood.

4. What was that like for you, to feel like you were responsible for my mood?

Not fun. A lot of times, the kids were coming to me and going, "What's wrong with Dad?" or "What's up with him?" and I'd be like, "I don't know." Sometimes it would be . . . I don't know that you need to put this in the book . . . but sometimes it would be like, "I know we had sex last night, so it's not on me. Whatever's wrong with him is not on me." Because sometimes if you really wanted to and I didn't, you would be in this pouty mood until I "fixed" things. So, if I fixed it and you still weren't better, then I'd be like, "I don't know."

5. **How has the change affected our sex life?**

   I no longer feel pressure to give in or feel guilty for not responding positively to hints or pressure for sex. Quite often, I felt like a vehicle or tool for you to get what you wanted, which wasn't me, but what you could get from me. Now, it's about the connection and both of us wanting to be together, which makes it a thousand times better.

6. **When thinking about all we've learned about intimacy, how has the change influenced or changed you?**

   It's hard to separate that from basic recovery principles. I'm certainly less of a doormat in my life. I'm willing to speak up and say something, which I really wouldn't have done very much of with you before. I know we had our arguments and stuff, but I kept things in for a long time versus just talking things through and being heard.

7. **When you consider my definition of *intimacy* presented in this book, which area has been the hardest or toughest for you to regularly give yourself to in relationships?**

   The ability to openly share feelings without the fear of rejection.

8. **Why do you think that is?**

Sometimes openly sharing your feelings can come with confrontation or other things, and I don't like confrontation.

9. **How has our pursuing intimacy with each other, and with friends and family, influenced our children?**

I think the whole process, the entire last seven years, we've had better tools to share with them when they have issues. I think some of it's just kind of seeing us or the change in us that has been a kind of osmosis.

10. **Do you feel like we've been more open to encouraging them to share their feelings?**

I think for the most part we always have. I just think that they're more likely to do that now because in the past, they were always worried about "What is Dad going to do with that? Is he going to get mad?" or whatever. So, I think they hid some things growing up. Now that our kids are older, and they've seen the changes in us, they have a much deeper relationship with us. They've also been able to cultivate some deeper relationships with others.

As you can probably tell, some of that was hard for me to hear. But it was important for me to hear. Despite that, it was far harder for those around me to live through. Had I implemented what I've learned over the past nine years much sooner in life, I would have spared my immediate family and others a lot of hurt and pain. Still, all has not been lost. All is not lost. God is a God of redemption. He is redeeming us! As Tammy noted, she and I are totally different today than we once were, as individuals and as married partners. Our children differ, too, from who they once were.

Wherever you are in the process of walking in intimacy, today can be the day you choose to take steps toward intimacy, no matter how big or how small. Your life and others' lives will be all the better. Begin today!

NEXT STEP

You've read and hopefully learned a lot about intimacy in this book. In fact, you may feel overwhelmed. Your next step is to be kind to yourself. Day by day, seek to apply the principles outlined in this book. Seek to be a little better tomorrow than the day before. One day, you, like me, will look back and note the incredible changes for the better that occurred in both your life and your relationships. One follow-up step to consider: read the next section for ways you can continue to grow and connect with others seeking to grow in intimacy.

Wrapping Things Up

Thank you for buying this book and for reading it. My sincere hope is that you found help that enables you to have greater intimacy in all your relationships. As I bring the book to a close, I want to provide some additional action steps you can take to continue changes you may have begun. Here are several options to consider:

- Become an Intimacy Fan by signing up at **www.RedefiningIntimacy.org** and receive biweekly emails with practical tips on how to become more intimate in your relationships.

- Bless the pastor of your church with a copy or two of *Redefining Intimacy*. It might surprise you to learn that very few pastors have ever taken a course specifically on the subject of intimacy—despite how important it is in our relationship with God. Many pastors don't know where to turn, and virtually every pastor is dealing with congregants who are experiencing marital difficulty. This book could be a huge resource for your pastor.

- Speaking of your church, are you involved in a church small group? Why not encourage your small group to do a study of *Redefining Intimacy*? You could cover a chapter a week and engage in discussion about the various things that stood out as members read. This might be the perfect way to transform the group into a more intimate one.

- Recommend that your church host a "What Is Intimacy?" seminar. What Is Intimacy? is a nonprofit ministry I lead designed to help people grow in intimate relationships with God and others. If your church hosts one of these, you'll hear from me personally as I expand on the principles and topics in this book. Plus, you'll have an opportunity to ask me questions directly. There are multiple ways I can engage with churches, including hosting full-day seminars, preaching at revivals or retreats, and being a guest speaker at marriage conferences and similar events. More information is available at **www.whatisintimacy.org**. I'd love to connect with you in person at a speaking engagement at your church.

- Finally, although it's not free, I have the ability, on a case-by-case basis, to coach men to become more intimate with those they care about. If you are interested in learning more, send me an email at **info@RedefiningIntimacy.org** and we can schedule a time to discuss the possibilities.

A HUGE ASK

Please help me.

I can't thank you enough for buying my book. If you have enjoyed it and found it to be of value, I'd like to ask for your help. I know it's a big ask, but there is no way *Redefining Intimacy* will be successful and get into the hands of people who really need to read it without a significant percentage of readers helping me in one of several ways. Would you please consider doing one of the following?

- Go online to one or more of the *Redefining Intimacy* booksellers or book review sites and write a positive review (a 5-star rating would be a blessing). Specifically, it would mean the world to me if you'd visit Amazon, Barnes & Noble, and Goodreads to share your positive review. Thank you in advance!

- Tell your pastor and other church leaders about the book and recommend that they purchase it. (Quick note: Many pastors live on a very tight income. Please consider buying them a copy. If funds are too tight for your pastor or church leaders, would you consider taking up a collection toward copies for them?)

- If you by chance are seeing a professional counselor or psychiatrist, tell them about the

book and ask them if they would like a free copy
for their consideration. They can email me at
info@RedefiningIntimacy.org to have one
sent to them. My hope is that it will become
a resource they can use and recommend to
others they are working with.

Blessings to you for your consideration and your help
in promoting real intimacy!

Rob Gion, Jr.

Bibliography

Bowlby, John. "The Nature of the Child's Tie to His Mother." *International Journal of Psycho-Analysis* 39, no. 5 (September/October 1958): 350–73. PMID: 13610508.

Cloud, Henry. "Learn How to Transform Your Relationships through Empathy." Video. Accessed June 24, 2024. https://youtube.com/watch?v=6UxFu31jMU0/.

Cloud, Henry, and John Townsend. *Safe People*. Grand Rapids, MI: Zondervan, 1995.

Cohen, Sheldon, Denise Janicki-Deverts, Ronald Turner, and William Doyle. "Does Hugging Provide Stress-Buffering Social Support? A Study of Susceptibility to Upper Respiratory Infection and Illness." *Psychological Science* 26, no. 2 (2015), 135–47. https://doi.org/10.1177/0956797614559284.

"Emotions List & Emotional Literacy." Six Seconds. Accessed June 14, 2024. https://www.6seconds.org/emotional-intelligence/topics/emotions-list/.

"The 500 Greatest Songs of All Time." *Rolling Stone*, February 16, 2024. https://www.rollingstone.com/music/music-lists/best-songs-of-all-time-1224767/.

"Forgiveness: Your Health Depends on It." Johns Hopkins Medicine, November 1, 2021. Accessed June 14, 2024. https://www.hopkinsmedicine.org/health/wellness-and-prevention/forgiveness-your-health-depends-on-it.

"Genetics vs. Genomics Fact Sheet." National Human Genome Research Institute. Accessed June 14, 2024. https://www.genome.gov/about-genomics/fact-sheets/Genetics-vs-Genomics.

Huecker, Martin, Kevin King, Gary Jordan, and William Smock. "Domestic Violence." National Library of Medicine, National Center for Biotechnology Information. April 9, 2023. https://www.ncbi.nlm.nih.gov/books/NBK499891/.

Inagaki, Tristen, and Naomi Eisenberger. "Neural Correlates of Giving Support to a Loved One." *Psychosomatic Medicine* 74, no. 1 (January 2012): 3–7. doi: 10.1097/PSY.0b013e3182359335. Epub 2011 Nov 9. PMID: 22071630.

Johnson, Spencer. *Who Moved My Cheese? An A-Mazing Way to Deal with Change in Your Work and in Your Life.* New York: Putnam Adult, 1998.

Koole, Sander, Mandy Tjew A Sin, and Iris Schneider. "Embodied Terror Management: Interpersonal Touch Alleviates Existential Concerns among Individuals with Low Self-Esteem." *Psychological Science* 25, no. 1 (2014): 30–37. https://doi.org/10.1177/0956797613483478.

Miller, Donald. *Scary Close: Dropping the Act and Finding True Intimacy.* Nashville: Nelson Books, 2015.

Mróz, Justyna, and Kinga Kaleta. "Forgive, Let Go, and Stay Well! The Relationship between Forgiveness and Physical and Mental Health in Women and Men: The Mediating Role of Self-Consciousness." *International Journal of Environmental Research and Public Health* 20, no. 13 (June 26, 2023): 6229. doi: 10.3390/ijerph20136229. PMID: 37444077; PMCID: PMC10341467.

Packheiser, Julian, Helena Hartmann, Kelly Fredriksen, Valeria Gazzola, Christian Keysers, and Frédéric Michon. "A Systematic Review and Multivariate Meta-analysis of the Physical and Mental Health Benefits of Touch Interventions." *Nature Human Behaviour* 8 (April 8, 2024): 1088–1107. https://doi.org/10.1038/s41562-024-01841-8.

Parrott, Les, and Leslie Parrott. *Saving Your Marriage before It Starts.* Grand Rapids, MI: Zondervan, 2006.

Phenomenon. Directed by Jon Turteltaub. Touchstone Pictures, 1996.

"Post-Traumatic Stress Disorder." National Institute of Mental Health, May 2024. Accessed June 19, 2024. https://www.nimh.nih.gov/health/topics/post-traumatic-stress-disorder-ptsd.

Sinek, Simon. *Start with Why: How Great Leaders Inspire Everyone to Take Action.* New York: Portfolio, 2009.

Turner, Tina. "What's Love Got to Do with It." *Private Dancer.* Hollywood, CA: Capitol Records, 1984.

Uvnäs-Moberg, Kerstin, Linda Handlin, and Maria Petersson. "Self-Soothing Behaviors with Particular Reference to Oxytocin Release Induced by Non-noxious Sensory Stimulation." *Frontiers in Psychology* 5 (January 12, 2015): 1529. doi: 10.3389/fpsyg.2014.01529.

"What Is Posttraumatic Stress Disorder (PTSD)?" American Psychiatric Association, November 2022. Accessed June 14, 2024. https://www.psychiatry.org/patients-families/ptsd/what-is-ptsd.

Yancey, Philip. *The Jesus I Never Knew.* Grand Rapids, MI: Zondervan, 1995.